TOES IN THE WATER

TOES IN THE WATER

STORIES OF LIVES CHANGED BY WILD SWIMMING

EDITED BY RACHEL JONES

Vertebrate Publishing, Sheffield
www.adventurebooks.com

TOES IN THE WATER

Edited by Rachel Jones

First published in 2023 by Vertebrate Publishing.

VERTEBRATE PUBLISHING, Omega Court, 352 Cemetery Road, Sheffield S11 8FT, United Kingdom. *www.adventurebooks.com*

A CIP catalogue record for this book is available from the British Library.

ISBN: 978-1-83981-188-3 (Paperback)

ISBN: 978-1-83981-189-0 (Ebook)

10 9 8 7 6 5 4 3 2 1

Vertebrate Publishing is committed to printing on paper from sustainable sources.

MIX
Paper | Supporting
responsible forestry
FSC® C018072
FSC
www.fsc.org

Printed and bound in Great Britain by Clays Ltd, Elcograf S.p.A.

CONTENTS

MENTAL HEALTH

For my family

INTRODUCTION

RACHEL JONES

When you are stomping up the river, along a path where the puddles have frozen and even the spiders' webs look like glittery Christmas decorations, there is a small voice in the back of your head, seriously questioning your life choices. Other people are probably still in bed, all cosy, or drinking coffee in a civilised fashion, not getting themselves covered in mud, skidding across puddles and stripping down to a cossie before chucking themselves into the water in the name of fun.

I am not sure what pushed me towards swimming in rivers. I had been suffering for a long time with an autoimmune disease which had really robbed me of a decent quality of life. I felt a deep yearning for *something* to help me feel well, but I didn't know what. I still feel so grateful that I found wild swimming and everything that comes with it. My life is now rich with the benefit of mini-adventures. I have found the most wonderful and supportive community that I have ever come across. We have howled with laughter together, and also cried together – the healing powers of the water seeming like the most perfect way to live through our feelings and also honour them by giving ourselves space to really feel them, in a world where quick fixes are much more popular. The friends I have made will, I am sure, be lifelong. Nothing binds you together like trying to get dressed in a gale or chasing your one remaining water shoe down a river in a fast-flowing current. I have seen the absolute best of people, and what we can do when we come together to achieve good things.

Wild swimming has also blessed me with the privilege of seeing the seasons change in the most intimate way. I felt the change in the air this year as summer shifted into autumn. I have grown to love seeing the swell of the seasons, and the environment around where we swim. I feel fiercely protective of these beautiful places – and have for the first time as an adult become involved in conservation work. The natural world has inspired me, and I promise you that seeing bats swoop down to feed at dusk, or a kingfisher zoom across the water, feels like a literal piece of magic that very few are able to see. It has been life-changing for me to be able to be a part of this world – not only does it place my own human trials into perspective, but I feel like I can now really *see* the beauty which is around me, a cathedral built from trees and clouds, and there is nothing more beautiful.

While my physical health has improved from swimming, the most pronounced benefit has been the improvement to my mental health. I have struggled with depression and anxiety my entire life, and now, for the first time, I have breaks where I do not feel like that any more. I am able to do more, and be more, and I feel that my inelegant dunking (I am a clumsy so-and-so!) is the root of this positive change.

All these things, all this positive change in my life, I would wish for you too. On my way to becoming an avid wild swimmer, I have done a lot of learning and being inspired by other swimmers – folks who I have slurped back hot chocolate with, and folks I have never met but whose work has fed my passion via social media. This book is a compendium of works by wonderful swimmers who contribute to our community and help us keep the joy of swimming alive. There are three main themes in this book, around community, the environment and mental health: all the things that have really struck a chord with me over my swimming life-span. I invite you to slip into their beautiful and inspiring stories, just like you would slip into a cool river. Relish every second of the journey, and take the time to celebrate what resonates with you. We are all so lucky to have found wild swimming – I am grateful for it and for all of you every day.

COMMUNITY

ANNA DEACON
A SENSE OF BELONGING

I hardly slept, my body jerking awake roughly once an hour, worrying I would sleep through the multiple alarms I had set. My kit, all laid out the night before, was scooped up as I crept quietly through the house so I didn't wake the family, or the dog! I filled my flask with hot coffee and did a final check that I had everything. The car was covered in a thick frost, which I tried to quietly scrape away in the dark so as not to wake the neighbours. I picked up friends as we went, and as I drove down towards Portobello Beach in Edinburgh I could see the sky beginning to lighten just a touch and the butterflies in my tummy began to flutter in earnest.

We arrived at the shore and already around fifty women were huddled in small groups, quietly chatting and laughing. As we stood there, more and more arrived, a steady flow of dryrobes, IKEA bags, bobble hats and huge smiles. It was International Women's Day 2022 and over 700 souls joined us there on that beach.

In 2019 we organised a swim gathering on International Women's Day, a sunrise swim to fit in with everyone's work schedules; we met new friends and old and swam in a glorious happy pod of around forty people. In 2020 we decided it was such fun, why not make it a bit bigger and use the moment to raise money for women's charities, in particular our local Women's Aid? We spoke to groups across the UK and beyond who joined us that day, and between us we raised thousands upon thousands. Then, the following week, lockdown struck. That was the last big swim for all of us. The hugs, shared drinks and snacks were suddenly outlawed; even swimming was officially not allowed on our local beaches. Just like that, our community seemed to vanish.

Except it didn't. During lockdown, the outdoor-swimming community grew and grew across the UK and, while not in large groups, it was like a slow gathering of momentum. So 2022 came around and that moment, standing on the shore watching these 700 people arrive to swim together, was the most incredible feeling of a reunion of sorts, a huge swimming tribe finally in the water at the same time.

We stood in silence and remembered those who had lost their lives to violence, those in the Ukraine and those we had lost, with hands clasped, arms comforting, eyes closed.

Then the Zumba warm-up began – and the squeals as the first swimmers dipped their toes in the extremely cold North Sea. I waded into the water with tears filling my eyes as I looked around at this mass of amazing people, this tribe of swimmers. Some faces I knew and hugged tight after a long time, some I recognised from the beach, some I had never seen before. All were smiling, bobbing about, jumping, and utterly filled with joy on every level.

The sun finally popped up from the horizon in a huge fiery ball, and the already-pink sky flooded us with a golden light and created a beautiful red-hued pathway in the water. The swimmers cheered at the sun, and this moment, this incredible moment of solidarity in the water, was something I shall never ever forget: swimming in a freezing cold soup of swimmers, surrounded by golden light and laughter.

All day long, I was sent photographs and messages from others who had been a part of it; the notifications when donations were sent pinged incessantly on my phone – we raised over £9,000 in total that day, spread across three local women's charities.

Since moving to Edinburgh from London in 2016 and building a new life for my family here, I had found it harder than ever to make new friends – being freelance and working from home, with my kids at the older end of primary school, there just wasn't chance. I felt so lost for a long time and, while I had my family nearby and a small handful of friends, I didn't feel part of a community. I started swimming regularly with my cousin and eventually joined a local swim group online, but still felt too nervous to actually go and swim with anyone. But when someone posted about swimming at the tiny beach five minutes from my home, I decided to pluck up the courage and go along. A handful of us met on the shore, a little uncertain as we had never seen anyone swim there before. We had a lovely first swim and started swimming together regularly from then, and more people joined us and the group grew until January 2020, when there were around forty people who were in the Facebook group and between five and fifteen who came regularly to the beach for a swim. It was a safe little community; all ages and walks of life came together to swim, encourage one another and often chat with a hot drink, a cake and a fire afterwards.

Covid blew all that up. Our little community dispersed – we weren't allowed to swim, let alone meet on the beach. But a funny thing happened: the requests to join the group started to flow in and once the beaches were fair game again, they seemed to be packed with swimmers. It seemed many pool swimmers were missing their regular swims and wanted to keep up their training, and the fine summer weather helped. Most parks, beaches and outdoor beauty spots were packed with people. I thought numbers would fall off once the temperatures dipped, except they didn't – they grew more. On my daily morning walks on the shore with the dog, I was seeing small groups swimming every single day; they were there at other times of the day too. Our group grew from 40 to 2,500, and this seems to be the case in swimming groups throughout the UK. People were finding outdoor swimming and then – after realising the joy, adventure and community – they stayed. Many people cancelled their gym memberships for good, preferring the sea to the pool; others started run/swim groups, mental health groups, men's groups, long-distance training groups, swimming lessons, mothers' groups … and it just continues to grow.

So what is it about the water that brings us together? What is it that binds us swimmers and creates these bonds? When Vicky Allan and I were writing our wild-swimming books, our focus was on the people, why they swam and what they loved about it; and one of the things that we kept coming back to was community: people love being part of something, they love bringing new swimmers into the fold, sharing their joy and their love of the water with others. Swimming is a leveller; when you strip down to your swimsuit and enter freezing cold water, it doesn't matter a jot what job you have, where you live, how old you are, what you look like ... all of that is stripped away and everyone is just the same: cold and exhilarated. You can't really focus on much else, especially swimming through the winter, when you must focus on staying safe and not getting too cold and know when to come out. This is something I hear time and time again from swimmers we have interviewed for our books, or people we chat with on the shores of any swim spot. It can give you a closeness with others that is hard to come by in other ways, sharing a cold swim, experiencing the freezing pain of that first immersion and then the joy that follows, splashing in the waves, whooshing down a river, standing under a waterfall – all visceral experiences that are hard to explain to anyone who wasn't there doing it too.

We must look out for one another: it is a risky business at times and keeping an eye out for other swimmers is something that we all do. Helping someone out who has maybe stayed in too long with an extra layer or a hug; holding the hand of a first-timer; advising on kit to someone with freezing toes admiring your neoprene booties; sharing a drink with someone struggling to warm up; organising swims for beginners so they are aware of the tides, cold, dangers and so on.

Outdoor swimmers are a friendly bunch. We have travelled all over the UK and Ireland meeting swimmers for our books, and without fail have been met with immediate warmth and friendship. We have been struck by how many groups have also organised fundraisers for charities that meant a lot to them, with people doing swim challenges like swimming every day in February, or organising large group swims with donation buckets, mass skinny dips, yoga and swim, full-moon swims, fancy-dress swims. You name it, someone is doing it and raising money for charities at the same time. We can be a force for big change as a swimming community.

Post-lockdown, there has been a huge surge in mental health swimming groups, notably the Mental Health Swims community, who have swim leaders on practically every beach and lake across the UK now taking new swimmers and experienced swimmers alike into the water and providing a safe place for them to talk about their mental health. So many of us find that swimming provides a relief from stress, anxiety and depression, and the science really appears to back this up, so it is no surprise to me that these groups continue to grow and thrive and are providing such a safe space for many people at a time when mental health services are at breaking point. Notably in our local area, there is a fabulous new men's swim group which is a growing community of men who meet to talk about their mental health and swim together; it has become a real lifeline to so many. There is also a lovely group for new mums who leave their children in a nearby creche and all come to the beach for a mindfulness session, a group chat and a swim led by a wonderful local charity. These groups are springing up constantly and I am beyond delighted every time I hear about them. Our community is plugging a gap that the mental health services are unable to cope with and is providing vital resources.

Our community is also facing down the government, petitioning for cleaner water, taking action to clean our beaches and investigate microplastics in our waters. When you are swimming in the water, you become aware of what could be in it and how this just isn't okay. We are pressuring our local MPs and MSPs to prevent water companies from expelling sewage into our rivers and seas; swim groups across the UK are campaigning relentlessly and this has been picked up on the national news. Hopefully by keeping this pressure up, we can make change happen. Swimmers are often custodians of their swim spots, picking up litter others have left or that has been washed up by the sea. Many swimmers take part in mass litter-picking days organised by groups such as Surfers Against Sewage or the Marine Conservation Society, who also analyse the litter collected and use that data to put pressure on the government, which can in turn lead to the banning of single-use plastic items and collecting data about where the pollution is coming from. But also, many just pick up litter every time they visit the beach or river. There are also groups collecting samples of water in all sorts of swim spots and sending it off to be analysed for microplastics, and those collecting nurdles. Swimmers are at the forefront of so much of this pressure to clean up our waters, and our voices are starting to be heard.

For me, and for so many others, finding people to swim with in my local area has opened up a whole new world of community. New friends to bond with, causes to fight, a sense of belonging and purpose, a joy and love of our water bonded over wave-jumping, cake-sharing and advice-swapping. Swimming in a sea of 700 amazing, unique, like-minded people as we watched that red sun appear over the horizon, knowing we were all there to do something good together, was something I will never forget, and I doubt anyone there will either. This outdoor-swimming community is utterly fabulous – we are a force for good, for change, we are welcoming and friendly, we don't judge and we provide a safe space for many. We are connected through the water.

JOHNNY HARTNELL

WHEELIE BINS AND SWIMVENTURES

I've always been drawn to water. Even from a young age, you'd find me playing down the beck or skiving on a Tuesday to go fishing with Grandad Harry. There's just something about it, a magnetic pull, that draws me in. I never understood any greater meaning to it as a child; I just loved it. Pure, unfiltered joy. As I've grown older and my love for immersing myself in cold climes has continued, greater meaning has become apparent. It's not just a vat of liquid, a playground. It's a healer, a friend, a connection, a force greater than anything else that unites us all.

I try to get in the water most days for a moment of reflection. No matter what's going on in the world or how much of a rubbish day it may have been, when you take those first steps into the water, or dive in my case, everything else escapes your mind. In that moment, the world goes quiet, all noise – both inwardly and outwardly – is silenced, and nothing else matters. I find the experience of cold water unlike anything else. When I'm fully immersed in the icy raptures, it's just me and nature. Whether it's the mental reset you get from a solo dip or that special shared moment with like-minded individuals, the benefits are invaluable.

Until recently, I always swam alone or in small groups in local rivers. I am incredibly lucky to have such beautiful swim spots on my doorstep. The rivers Twiss and Doe in my village, Ingleton, are my regular haunts, accompanied by regular forays to the Lake District. From high tarns to Scottish shores, I try to swim wherever I go. I am never without my trunks just in case – well, sometimes, but we won't go into that! The UK is home to some of the most incredible swim spots and I feel honoured to have dipped my toes into some real gems. My swimventures really have come full circle since my days of playing down the river as a child. The kids of the village, myself included, would always go to the salmon jumps in the summer, a spot that is now a matter of minutes from my doorstep and that still remains one of my favourite places to get my cold-water fix – although it would seem I'm the only one to frequent this spot in the winter, I can't think why! But it is fantastic.

When lockdown hit in 2020, my wild-swimming adventures came to a standstill along with the rest of the world. Although I was incredibly fortunate that I have a beautiful spot for swimming only yards from my front door, venturing further afield was not meant to be, so I racked my brains as to how I could make the best out of the situation and get that much-needed cold-water fix.

Now, I'll let you into a little secret. We all, unbeknown to us, have our very own swimming pool for one outside our homes. Mine is courtesy of Craven District Council. Our wheelie bin. Fill that bad boy up with ice-cold water (or lukewarm if you're new to the game) and hop in. It's the ideal solution when you're unable to get to the river, or if the waters are too high to safely dip. I named mine my 'isolation station' and, although it may have looked like insanity to others, it kept me sane during the craziest time of them all.

'Where's Dad?'
'He's in the bin!'

A CASUAL EXCHANGE IN THE HARTNELL
HOUSEHOLD C. 2020.

Binny dipping is now a great part of my swim routine. I often hop in for my morning brew (Yorkshire tea, of course), and it was an absolute lifesaver when I was partaking in the January Daily Dip.

The January Daily Dip was started by two swim friends, Sonya and Jamima, from Todmorden. They wanted to raise money and awareness for Crisis, a charity fighting to end homelessness in the UK. The event involves venturing into cold water every day in January to face the freeze and, ultimately, help to end homelessness. Jamima, who I met through wild swimming, asked if I would like to join them in their mission, and of course I accepted. I started in 2021, completed my second January Daily Dip in 2022, and I would like to try to do this every January. It is not a heroic sporting challenge but a daily vigil into the cold to remember and raise awareness that far too many people don't have the privilege of a lovely warm home to return to. This is a huge crisis in the UK, with over 220,000 families and individuals experiencing the worst forms of homelessness.

After starting out with only three people, there is now a team of over thirty dippers venturing into the icy January waters in nothing but their swimmers and a smile. To date it has raised over £100,000 to help homeless and displaced individuals. I feel honoured to be a part of such a fantastic mission.

Through wild swimming I have met some of the most incredible, inspiring people and made friends for life. The water brings people from all walks of life together. I've found wild swimming to be a true leveller. When you're in the water, you are united, all on the same playing field. When you're in the water, particularly if you're by a waterfall, you have this moment where you truly realise that there is something in the universe greater than us all and that we are all on this crazy ride together.

Wild swimming has become increasingly popular over the last few years as people discover its incredible benefits. With social media constantly growing and becoming ever more powerful, groups have been popping up in every corner of the globe to connect swimmers and join people through their love for cold water. I might be biased but one of the most welcoming groups out there is the Dales Dippers, based in the heart of the Yorkshire Dales. I met the fabulous gentlemen that are Stuart Gledhill and Les Peebles through sharing our beautiful local swim spots on social media. Without wild swimming, I would never have met them, and now we are inseparable and feel as though we have known each other forever: three peas in a totally bonkers but blooming brilliant pod. We decided to create the Dales Dippers, a Facebook group bringing swim-mad lads and lasses together, just as swimming had joined us. When we first created the page, we thought it would be incredible if we could reach 100 members, and now, a few years down the line, there are over 8,000 dippers in the group! It has allowed like-minded individuals to connect, share some of the Dales' most beautiful hidden gems and create a community of swim friends who look out for one another both in and out of the water. A typical Dales Dippers meet is finished with a flask of hot chocolate and some delicious home-made cake – what's not to love, eh?

I'm always singing the joys of wild swimming, and when talking about it to my girls, particularly in the colder months (which tend to be most of them here in sunny Yorkshire), I'm usually met with a resounding chorus of 'Dad, you're bonkers!' But on one occasion, rather spontaneously (and after a few sherbets at the pub), they decided they would join me the next day on my very early morning swim adventure for the summer solstice.

We all awoke bleary-eyed at 3 a.m. with an excited buzz, the kind you get when you're up at silly o'clock to head on holiday. Swimmers on, hot chocolate made in the flask and we were good to go! We hopped in the car and drove towards the breaking dawn and the Lake District. We met a fellow swim sister at Millerground on the edge of Windermere, ready to hit the water at precisely 4.32 a.m. as the sun rose to welcome in the longest day of the year. The water sat still, reflecting the dappled sky like a mirror on its surface, melting into beautiful ripples as we all took the plunge. A sense of hopeful tranquillity enveloped us all and, for a few moments, the world stood still. Staring up at the milky sky, getting brighter each second as the solstice sun crept through the clouds, we could hear nothing but the sounds of nature.

It's often a bustling spot, particularly in the summer, so to experience the lake in such a peaceful state was truly incredible. Just us and nature. It was magic. We chatted as a family, taking it all in. As the chaos of life wraps us up so often, it's rare to get a moment of peace all together, so sharing this moment will forever be one of my most treasured dips.

To anyone thinking about starting wild swimming, I'd say, just do it. If you've ever stood on a riverbank watching people wild swimming and thought, 'I'd love to do that, but I'm not sure I'm brave enough' or 'I don't know where to start', all us swim friends started somewhere and have been in your position before. Look for swimming groups in your local area. Check out the Outdoor Swimming Society website. There is a small section about swimming groups based in the UK and there is bound to be one very close to you!

Never swim alone when you're starting out. Always go with a friend or an organised group. Water is a force far greater than us all, so safety is key. Have a little browse on social media and you will be able to find a swim guide who can assist you on your journey into cold water. If you're visiting the Dales, then I would recommend seeking out my fellow Dales Dipper Les Peebles, an experienced swim guide. We always welcome new faces to the Dales Dippers and love nothing more than being a part of the start of someone's swim experience. And did I mention cake? Us wild swimmers love nothing more than something deliciously indulgent after a dip, and it's a well-known fact that after an icy-cold dip, cake is calorie-free. Billy bonus!

Try not to overthink things – the niggling worries of 'It's too cold' or 'I don't know if I can' are all just in your head. It really is a case of mind over matter. Be sure to go carefully and ease yourself in at first whilst you adjust to the temperatures. I always recommend starting out in the warmer months, then working towards the winter freeze. Once you're in, you'll be addicted, wanting every swim to be colder than the last. I'm thermometer crazy – I never dip without it now!

But, most importantly, remember to enjoy yourself. Smile and take it all in. It sounds so clichéd, saying that it'll change your life. But, trust me, it will.

BETH PEARSON
THE OSS COMMUNITY

Sometimes it takes two weeks on holiday or a passing encounter with the sublime to liberate one's thinking about life. Sometimes all it takes is a swim on a stormy night. On the night before Halloween in 2005, Kate Rew and Kari Furre drove eight hours from Somerset to the Lake District, accompanied for the entire journey by a wet concrete sky. 'We could go for a swim when we get there,' Kate suggested, with still an hour to go. The rationale was that while tedium, boredom and frustration can be taken with you on a trip, they can never outlast a swim. After standing in a puddle by the boot of the car to put on their wetsuits, the clouds throwing rain in their faces, they swam around a headland of Buttermere, the water black until dipping underneath revealed white pebbles, a sudden shelf; they cautiously stuck to the shore in the ominous conditions. Somewhere between this fifteen-minute adventure and the après-swim warmth of a peach dado rail and damask apricot curtains in a £25-per-night B&B came an epiphany: why not start an Outdoor Swimming Society?

In 2005 – seventeen years ago – people did swim outdoors in the UK, but they were largely old-timers who had swum outdoors since youth, or were considered somewhat eccentric outliers to 'normal' indoor pool swimmers. Outdoor swimming diminished in mainstream popularity sometime after the heyday of outdoor bathing during the Victorian era. Lidos had been filled in or sat empty, in gloomy states of disrepair.

People still swam the Channel, of course, and took part in elite open-water swims. However, there was little in the way of a community of purely recreational and amateur outdoor swimmers: no events, few local groups, and little authoritative knowledge about where to swim, how to do it, and what to be aware of. Of course, there is nothing wrong with being an eccentric outlier: the Outdoor Swimming Society merely proposed that eccentric outliers could all get together and perhaps encourage other eccentric outliers to get in the water. And, in doing so, make outdoor swimming socially acceptable again.

The first event was Breastrokes, a one-mile swim in Windermere and the Serpentine to raise money for breast cancer charities. As a starting point, Kate recalls, 'It was perfect: practically every time we went swimming, people yelled, "Are you doing this for charity?" at us from the banks, particularly on the Thames.' The Windermere mile was waymarked by a hot-chocolate stop at Silver Holme Island, which acted both as a necessary refreshment and a statement of intent: swimming outdoors didn't have to be about endurance, or speed, or time – it could be about just going for the experience. Feeling fresh or salt water on your skin. Looking around you. Noticing seasonal changes. Returning to the shore with the feeling that you'd been away for longer than you knew you had. Breastrokes attracted a lot of media coverage, purely on the basis of its novelty (and in spite of its deliberate misspelling). The momentum continued into the summer of 2006 with stealth swims at the Big Chill Festival, a Breastival swim at Bestival, full-moon swims on the Thames and an initiative to 'take a friend river-swimming'. OSS membership soared to 300. People wrote us letters: 'Thanks for giving me an identity. Before, I was just the odd bloke in the office who swam in rivers; now, I'm a "wild swimmer".'

Each subsequent year saw new adventures, events and increasingly overt political statements. The Big Jump event saw swimmers across Europe leap into a river at the same time on the same day. The OSS held a weekend event with swims around Burgh Island and down the Avon estuary (the latter would become the Swoosh). There were stunt swims at the Innocent Village Fete in Regent's Park and a protest at Rickmansworth Aquadrome, where swimming had been prohibited. In 2007, a core group of the OSS went on a swim tour around the UK to research spots for Kate Rew's iconoclastic *Wild Swim* book, which would be published the following year. The Derwent 10k would follow, along with Facebook-organised 'social swims'. From the OSS perspective, the group was developing a 'secure reputation for doing it our own way or being hippies'. Yet sometimes it takes an outsider to put their finger on what's really going on. The December Dip at Parliament Hill Lido saw participants swimming two widths of the pool in a water temperature of 4 °C. It was well attended by the press for its novelty value as well as the appearance of the Olympic open-water swimmer Cassie Patten, who would go on to run swim clinics with the OSS. Her father remarked to the camera as the swimmers dried off and compared goosebumps: 'I don't see a normal person here; they've all got mad glints in their eyes.'

What was building here? It was a movement. Although serendipity and impulse had played an important role in the genesis of the OSS, it had always been underpinned by a social purpose and some key organising features and people. An early statement of these reads as follows:

We believe it's time to get back to the joy of swimming under an open sky. Water needs no roof! Our manifesto:

- *We believe swimmers have too long been held in chlorinated captivity! Everyone with a set of bathers should be set free to immerse themselves in nature.*
- *We support all those keeping lidos open and lakes and rivers clean.*
- *We promise to enlarge and celebrate the beauty of every day we can by going for a nice outdoor swim.*
- *We pledge to take our friends with us so they can join.*
- *We embrace the rejuvenating effects of cold water and undertake to strip and dip wherever we can.*

While the initial aim of the OSS was to give people permission to swim outdoors, this was inevitably accompanied by a second, related goal: to share the swim love. To normalise outdoor swimming through social swimming events, connecting swimmers on social media platforms and, in so doing, democratise the use of the waterways of the UK and beyond. As the take-up of outdoor swimming accelerated, so did the ambition of OSS events and the organisation. We appointed regional representatives in 2010 to lead social swims, and local groups began to be established on Facebook (requiring a hardworking group of volunteers to administer). The iconic Dart 10k had its maiden event in the same year, joined by the Swoosh in 2015 and the Hurly Burly – eight years in the making – in 2017. Working with our charity partner Level Water, these events secured swimming tuition for children with disabilities. Membership increased to 25,000.

By this point, the OSS website had developed into a hub for authoritative advice and information about outdoor swimming, as well as tales of adventure. Few outdoor swimmers will have escaped being met with the comment 'I remember when it was just called swimming.' But does pool swimming require checking tide times, understanding rips and currents, developing specific swimming techniques, a basic understanding of the physiology of cold-water shock or a working knowledge of public access laws? The range of articles in the 'Survive' section of the website are collaborative and community-generated, but also verified by experts and experience. We are also committed to sharing that knowledge for free – we do not charge for the use of our website, our e-journal *elsewhere* is free, our Facebook pages and Twitter and Instagram accounts are maintained by committed volunteers. It's democratic but also encourages individual responsibility.

Then something happened in 2020. We knew that our membership had been increasing for a while, and particularly expanding into Europe, North America and Australia. But when the Covid pandemic took hold and lockdowns were instituted across the UK and beyond, this gentle acceleration tipped into something else. With indoor swimming pools closed and lockdown bringing about an acute desire for open spaces, swimming spots became overrun. We took the difficult decision to close the Wild Swim Map, in a bid to avoid honeypots and environmental degradation. Many of our local swimming groups had to close to new members. Outdoor swimming had truly gone mainstream. We now have 100,000 members across all channels, with over half a million visitors to the OSS website (and wildswim.com) in 2020.

Mainstream media attention was a given, no longer because swimming outdoors was novel, but because so many readers of certain publications did it that it became an essential topic to cover. Companies selling outdoor-swimming-related products, including tow floats and wetsuits, started to sell out. Robes for changing after swims became so omnipresent in some areas that one brand became a byword for unwelcome groups of outdoor swimmers. Instagram accounts appeared featuring 'swimfluencers', sponsored to advertise branded products. There were moves to regulate and charge for swimming in venues that had always been free. Dippers, long-distance swimmers, Wim Hof devotees, fair weather dookers, cold-water aficionados, ice swimmers … it's now more unusual to meet people who *haven't* been outdoor swimming, or who don't at least say they would like to try it. Or, to paraphrase Cassie Patten's dad, outdoor swimmers no longer all have a mad glint in their eye.

For the OSS, this huge expansion in the number of people outdoor swimming and the attention of the media and commercial enterprises brought its own set of challenges. In one way, it felt like the original aims of the OSS had been achieved. In many others, it felt as if there was a risk of losing what it was all about. Faced with pressures to do otherwise, not expanding and not growing takes considerable effort. But as the self-declared 'international anti-governing body of outdoor swimming', we resist commercialisation, are naturally averse to bandwagons, and prioritise whatever maintains the soul of the modest pastime of taking your clothes off and stepping into a river, a lake or the sea. This means helping our inland access team to provide support, resources and a network to those interested in improving swimming access for inland waters. It means telling stories through our free monthly e-journal *elsewhere* and continuing to #sharetheswim love on Instagram, Facebook and Twitter. It means supporting the community through free access to authoritative articles in the Survive section of our website. It means continuing to provide a network for administrators of local outdoor-swimming groups, recognising that for many of us, a local and often creatively named group provided us with a warm welcome and an introduction to outdoor swimming.

Now we have more than 100,000 members, to what extent can this be described as a community? Well, the OSS community has always been one of loose ties. For every semi-institutionalised local swimming group with a schedule and something like a hierarchical structure, there is a local swimming spot where individuals come and go, sometimes coinciding, sometimes not. There are still more who pop in and make a unique page impression on our website in ways that we will never understand, nor attempt to. Who is reading 'Wild Swims in Wharfedale', which was our most-read feature for ten years? Who knows. But we hope they all had a great time. Similarly, the passing years have seen many great, committed and enthusiastic outdoor swimmers pass through the OSS as volunteers and directors, each becoming part of the story and community of what outdoor swimming means today. As co-founder and former director Kari Furre puts it: 'On reflection, the swimming is just there, feeding into everything else. I am a time-served amateur, who didn't know she was part of a movement.'

ELLA FOOTE

STRENGTH FROM STRANGERS

The rain was lashing against my simple raincoat. The red, jacket-style design was made for a light shower in an urban area, not for boat trips off the west coast of Scotland. The sea simmered beneath the hull, bubbling and boiling. I was on a small fishing boat with a group of almost strangers and we were heading out to the Gulf of Corryvreckan, a narrow strait between the islands of Jura and Scarba, in Argyll and Bute.

The Corryvreckan is the third-largest whirlpool in the world. Strong Atlantic currents and unusual underwater topography together produce a particularly intense tidal race in the Corryvreckan channel. As the flood tide enters the narrow area between the two islands, it speeds up and meets a variety of seabed features, including a deep hole and a rising pinnacle. These features combine to create whirlpools, standing waves and a variety of other surface effects. It was once believed to be unnavigable, and scuba divers describe it as the most dangerous dive in Britain. We were on our way to swim across it.

John Donald and I had met at Bray Lake near Maidenhead when I was training for a Channel relay crossing the year before. He had been signing in before entering the water and I recognised his name from an online swimming group we were both members of. We had an odd exchange, not really knowing each other at all, before he got in and swam off. We crossed paths a couple of times that year at lidos and lakes, but it was when I was swimming on New Year's Day at Parliament Hill Lido that the idea to swim across the Corryvreckan came about. I was in my thirtieth year and had an idea to complete thirty memorable swims to mark it. I was in deep avoidance; I wasn't happy at work, at home or in the relationship I was in. Swimming had become an escape from reality, and any suggestion of more swimming was always welcome.

John had been swimming to aid a back injury and addiction. He had found a community of swimmers at Parliament Hill Lido and suggested forming a group to travel to Scotland and swim the Gulf of Corryvreckan as one of my thirty swims. I laughed at the time. I hardly knew this man and I wasn't going to consider flying to Scotland with a bunch of strangers. I remember mentioning it to my boyfriend, hoping for at least a little concern about the idea, but he didn't seem to care either way. I ruminated on the idea for a while and then forgot all about it until John got in touch. He had it all planned out: swimmers, a support boat, flights and somewhere to stay. I just had to say yes. It seemed totally bananas – I didn't even know if I was good enough to swim the distance – but I found myself booking my flight that day.

I travelled with John and his friend Jeremy. They seemed to be close mates. When we got to Glasgow airport, I met seven more swimmers, most from Cambridge, and we embarked on a car journey to the west coast. I had briefly visited Edinburgh once, but this was my first experience of beautiful Scotland. I stared out of the window as we sped past glittering lochs, rolling mountains, flora and fauna. The rest of the group seemed to know each other better and, as we travelled, I heard stories and chats about solo Channel crossings, long-distance swimming achievements and challenges. I felt increasingly out of my depth.

On the day of the swim, the weather was awful. There was significant chop and, despite assurances that slack tide would make the swim safe and simple, I was worried. We swam in two pods, the faster and slower swimmers. We had two support boats, and a local seal had popped up to spectate. I don't remember much of the swim – it was bouncy and visibility was difficult. As the slowest swimmer, I just focused on the swimmers in front of me and tried not to think about the seal too much. I do remember gripping the edge of a stone and grassy surface on Scarba, clumps of grass in my hands and soil under my nails. I somehow made it across. The distance was short, but the sea felt significantly different from anything I had swum before.

With a long weekend still ahead of us, more swims were planned over lunch and I happily followed, giddy with swimming joy and from the friendships I had formed. I was told about swims in Cambridge and a three-river safari, which I was later invited to join as part of my swimming project. We swam in lochs, rivers and an old slate quarry. The water was always cool and clear, the conversation compelling and my companions entertaining. It was late one afternoon when Jeremy asked me about my life. I didn't know what to tell him. My relationship was in tatters, I lived alone and I had no idea where my career was going. I was deeply unhappy and hoping that somehow things would turn around. I remember telling Jeremy about my boyfriend and feeling hopeless. Jeremy put his hand on mine, firmly told me that my boyfriend's issues were not about me, and smiled at me in the knowledge that I had to stop looking to my partner to solve my unhappiness.

Not long after I returned from that trip, the relationship ended. I was heartbroken, but the swimming community picked me back up, dusted me off and set me on a new path. I went to Cambridge and met up with my fellow Corryvreckan swimmers, and they took me on their swim safari. We plunged into the River Cam from the Riverbank Club, where naked onlookers waved with encouragement, and whooshed out of a sluice gate into the River Nene. I felt reeds brush my legs and swam under bridges trying to avoid river trolls. I laughed: big belly laughs. The water washed away any tears and these people, this group of like-minded swimmers, gave me hope.

Growing up, my life wasn't that wild or connected to the outdoor world. I grew up on the edge of a greenbelt where I rode my bike and begrudgingly went on family walks after Sunday roasts, but my childhood was mostly urban. Summer holidays would include a week or two on the Dorset coast and we would collect shells, swim in the sea and look out at the horizon. It was peppered with wilder days, fishing for minnows and paddling about in a wooden rowboat at our friend's home in Lincolnshire. Occasionally, I would climb in the old cherry trees near home and we slept in a tent adjacent to my grandparents' caravan, but I never owned walking boots or proper outdoor gear. When I was about eleven, we went on an outdoor pursuits week with school. We rode ponies, hiked into a slate mine, went on a 'blind' walk in the dark and wore borrowed walking boots that we coated in dubbin each day. I picked up some outdoor skills I still use today, but most of what I have learnt I owe to the community of swimmers I have met over the past fifteen years.

I am still an amateur in the outdoors, despite endless efforts to educate myself better. I feel confident in all types of open water and have developed skills to teach, coach and guide others. But I still seek support from those around me. I feel no shame in asking fellow swimmers for help and advice. Before a recent trip to Finland, I didn't think twice about asking my friend Suzanna Cruickshank about decent boots for snow and ice. I am grateful for all I learnt through volunteering and supporting the Outdoor Swimming Society – I wouldn't know what to do when I encountered waterfalls and white water if it wasn't for Lynne Roper. I am fortunate enough to be able to lean on the community I have helped grow as well as still learn from. I have made mistakes, have had close encounters in the wild that could have gone a different way, but will always hold myself accountable and willing to learn from them. Through the seasons, all the weather and all the circumstances society and life throws at us, swimming has remained. Like the river flows, it is sometimes calm and easy, and at other times hard, fast and frightening.

There are plenty of swimmers who have swum further, harder, longer, colder or more adventurously, but I don't claim to be anything but someone who is striving, learning, discovering and open to all that is offered to me. I am aware how lucky I am that I can put on a swimsuit every day for some aspect of my career, but I worked hard to get here. I also owe a lot to the swimmers who swim beside me today. I have fantastic swimming cheerleaders. With every beautiful photo Roger Taylor takes, every video clip Bruno Teves captures and each friend who plunges in with me regardless, I am so thankful. The swimming community continues to teach, evolve and support me, and I am so happy for that.

CP ROBINSON

THE COAST IS QUEER

Why does the sea, a lake, a river, an unheated lido, the cold and open water feel so inherently queer? That's how it has always felt to me. It is a question I started to ask myself more and more when I was asked to contribute to this book and write about my experiences of open-water swimming as part of the LGBTQ+ community.

The folks who identify with the term 'queer' in some way challenge the social constructs of gender or sexual identity in their lives. My point is that they are radicals: in a world of hostile landowners and groups trying to block access to open water, companies and governments polluting rivers and the sea, and just generally most people thinking anyone who gets into water that cold is a bit bonkers – open-water swimmers are activists just by existing.

I started swimming in the sea as lockdowns were easing, and Dr Heather Massey – an amazing researcher – was looking at whether cold-water immersion could be physiologically proven to impact mental health and well-being. At the time, I was looking for community after having recently moved to the city I now call home – I wanted to embed myself and properly root in. With the help of some amazing coaches (shout-out to Bec Mason and Tori Stevens), I took a six-week introductory course to sea swimming; it was there that I met someone I'd now call my queer chosen-family sister.

To us, the sea, three times a week throughout the year, became a therapist's office. It was somewhere we gave each other relationship advice, shared career struggles, discussed the intersection (and not) of our politics, spoke about families and past trauma, lunch recipes, sewing patterns, spirituality, German culture, the best TikToks of the week, and of course honed the best techniques for rewarming love handles. Even before we started sea swimming, we were both activists; sea swimming just heightened our activism. Something about six-degree water on your genitals at 7 a.m. spurs a certain mentality of 'let's take on the world' – my swim buddy set up a local water pollution action group and I set up a queer activism campaign, both of us acting as an unofficial second in command to the other at protest events and community gatherings. We discovered an odd intersection here as well for crafting, and together have been the troubleshooter for each other's 'craftivism' – I stitched a fifteen-foot-wide intersex-inclusive pride flag for Portsmouth Pride and my swim buddy created a four-foot-wide realistic version of the poop emoji ... more on that later.

I advocate loudly for cold-water immersion and open-water swimming, due to the amazing effects it can have on physical and mental health. It's impacted me in ways that I didn't expect – I thought it would all be about connection to my natural environment, which it absolutely is as well. For people my age, and especially queer people my age, I don't know many who don't speak to a therapist or in some other way work on their own self-development, maturely express boundaries, continually develop communication skills and look properly at their own feelings. Open-water swimming became part of this for me, and added to the portfolio – or the layers – of my own self-driven mental health and well-being care. Writing this got me thinking about the importance that open-water swimming has played in keeping me safe and sane over these past few years, while life has handed me some challenges. I think knowing that this *can* happen is also part of the attraction for queer people, again in building up those layers of self-care ... and what's more, it's free and the queers do love a thrift!

The relationship I have formed with my swim buddy is far from unique – in speaking to other queer people who swim wild, I have found that these supportive relationships exist everywhere from duos like us to entire group communities. We're multiplying like hell, and you can find queers in the open water almost anywhere you go, if you know where to look. From the Trans Can Sport groups swimming in Brighton, the Merfolk Adventures in South Wales, and Cornwall Pride taking part in the regular Mental Health Swims series – LGBTQ+ wild-swimming groups are popping up all over the place.

What is it about open and wild water that attracts the queers? Does it give us a satisfaction in feeling like we're doing something we 'shouldn't' be doing, or does it connect us more to nature and our surroundings? Does it feel reminiscent of queer art from bygone eras idolising water, or does it give us community in sport without having to take us to the toxic memories of changing rooms and leisure centres?

I don't know about you, but I have such distinct memories of leisure centre swimming pools from the late 1990s – verruca socks, the eye-stinging levels of chlorine, vending machines with Discos and beige cups of soup – that going near a swimming pool isn't exactly the most attractive concept as a queer adult. And that's before we talk about the changing rooms, which for many queer people above a certain age elicit horrendous memories about body image, teasing and clique-culture. And that's just for cis-gender people (those who identify with the gender they were assigned at birth), before we move on to consider how those spaces feel for our trans community. This is why it's particularly interesting and important to speak about trans people and wild swimming, and to preface that by noting that I'm not a member of the trans community so I don't presume to speak on behalf of individual trans people, or the trans community as a whole. But from experiences I've had when swimming (primarily) in the sea with trans friends and members of our queer community, sea swimming environments and communities can prove to offer a completely different experience to that of pool swimming.

Pool swimming, especially as an adult without children, I'm sure nobody reading this will need telling, often feels like it's all about technique, speed, races, events, the right swimming costume, not to mention the changing facilities. Yet swimming in the open is all about the accomplishment of just getting your shoulders (or sometimes upper thighs) in the water, the connection to nature, floating in the current, the chat with anyone else daft enough to be out in the cold, fumbling to get your

T-shirt back on and getting a hot chocolate! So much of my experience of being around the queer community and open-water swimming has been about all of these things and wanting to find more people who want to do the same. I even had a trans friend say to me recently that they'd rather undress, swim and air dry on our local nudist beach than use our local university pool and their (by all accounts, relatively progressive, gender-neutral) facilities. Why? Because the coast is queer of course. Nobody is concerned with which changing rooms you're using, what costume you're wearing, whether your nipples are covered or not, overtaking you in a lane, following the straight line of tiles at the bottom of the pool, or choking on chlorine when you mistime a breath and someone storms past you (to paraphrase Victoria Wood) like a hairy torpedo in Lycra shorts!

In fact, one of my favourite things about wild swimming's post-lockdown boom has been the innovation in all the paraphernalia (I promise there's a point to this), and while I'm sure plenty of people are like me and don't need more targeted Instagram adverts for cool outdoor swim things because it's too good and makes us spend money, some amazing things come from it too. Namely in swimwear for all which has been amazing to see, and I've had the pleasure of seeing friends' confidence and attitude towards open-water swimming completely change once they were in swimwear that they were comfortable in with their body shape – whether trans or not.

Again, this isn't explicitly a change made for the queer community, but definitely one which attracts the queer community. Knowing that we have interesting choices to suit not only diverse body shapes but also just our style preferences is a big motivator when looking for an activity to take up as an adult.

I do have to bring us back now to the four-foot poop which was initially going to be towed around Portsea Island by boaters, swimmers and paddlers to mark a protest event against water companies dumping sewage in the sea. It ended up being the centrepiece to a community day of action – it had to be sawn in half to fit it out of the dining room where it was made, and we needed to beg/borrow/steal a Luton van to deliver it to site. Community, guerrilla, self-made, tongue-in-cheek, impactful ... queer and camp.

Perhaps that's why the coast is queer. Taking part in open-water swimming fulfils some of the basic needs of queer people: to connect with their community, to in some way make a change to the world, and to care for their own well-being.

PAULINE BARKER
THE POLAR BEAR CHALLENGE

A great philosopher once said, 'The whole is greater than the sum of the parts'. This phrase is attributed to Aristotle and, while there is nothing about metaphysics in the world of swimming, the synergy effect which he describes is very often evident in the way that immersion into cold water can touch lives in the most unexpected and joyful ways.

The benefits of cold-water swimming have long been known to our friends in the more snowy and cold regions of Europe and beyond, and the motto of the International Winter Swimming Association is 'The colder the water, the warmer the friendships.'

In the UK, cold-water swimming has really taken off and started to become popular over the last decade as more and more people become aware of the physical and mental benefits it brings and realise that it can be fun. It's often 'Type 2' fun, which is where we look back with a fond memory to what, at the time, may have felt like we were well out of our comfort zone, but then the memory of numb fingers and toes fades and we laugh at the remembrance of spilling hot chocolate everywhere because our hands were shaking the mug so much.

From the first tentative dip of a toe into water rather more chilly than we've been accustomed to, to a feeling akin to the high that runners may feel during a long, arduous run, the effect of cold water on the human body and psyche can be profound.

Of course, there is the sense of achievement that you feel from having pushed yourself out of your comfort zone, but it's more than just the swimming that draws people back time and again – it brings people together into a sense of community, whether that be an actual meetup with friends to enjoy the water or through social media and online inter-actions to share experiences with the wider world. It's the camaraderie and support that builds up within a group of people who know that what they're doing may (to drylanders) look to be just a little bit bonkers!

It's not something that appeals to everyone, but for those of us who choose to embrace the cold, we think that we're actually the sensible ones because there's a wealth of evidence – both anecdotal and proven – which shows that cold-water swimming can bring fantastic benefits to both physical and mental health.

It's often the case that a group of folk who swim together are as diverse as can be in their dryland lives, but the commonality of a lure towards the water sparks friendships that may never otherwise be formed as our paths would not normally cross. That can create a group dynamic of inclusivity because, no matter who you are, everyone is equal when in the water and you can leave the stresses of home, work, family or anything else behind and just savour the moment for yourself in your own way.

Cold-water swimming does seem to have a particular attraction for ladies, as there are far more women than men taking up the sport, although the gents are starting to catch up.

When I set up the Polar Bear Challenge in 2017, the idea was a simple one and the plan was to encourage myself and a few friends with a target to swim through the winter and have a bit of a celebration at the end. I know that everyone likes a bit of bling, and a sew-on badge is very reminiscent of days as a Girl Guide spent trying to acquire the necessary knowledge to be awarded one of the coveted badges, so I decided to go retro and offered everyone a badge and a medal as a reward.

It very quickly became apparent that I had hit upon a popular idea that caught the imagination of a lot of people, and four days later I had 250 swimmers in a Polar Bear posse all looking forward to completing a Winter Swimming Challenge. A simple plan to carry on swimming through the winter from November through to the end of March and commit to swimming 200 metres twice a month really took off.

Fast-forward to September 2021 and there are 4,500 swimmers from all over the world who have committed to this season's challenge, and twelve different challenges to choose from – including Penguins!

Swimming through the winter is a hard challenge. Whether you are a Polar Bear in just a swimsuit or choose to put on a few extra layers or some neoprene and become a Penguin, it is very daunting when you first put your toe in the water knowing full well it's going to be f-f-f-f-freezing! Here Rebecca demonstrates how cold-water swimming can really be a challenge to savour, as it helped to inspire her to keep swimming as part of her Covid recovery:

Although I've swum outdoors my whole life, I'd never swum a whole winter without any neoprene, so Polar Bear was a natural choice of challenge for me. I learnt a lot about my limits in the cold and it definitely kept me motivated to swim a good distance regularly for the whole winter. When I got Covid in the final month, the support and advice from the community helped me be patient with my recovery and ultimately complete the challenge. It's a well-designed and well-organised challenge and I'm proud of my shiny new Arctic Polar Bear badge!

REBECCA JOHNS

It's also a challenge that needs to be undertaken cautiously, as plunging into cold water does have its dangers, but there's plenty of help and advice both from myself and from other members of the community who have previous seasons' experience and know the pitfalls. Everyone shares their knowledge and that's a valuable part of the community.

Whether someone is starting out in their first season as a Penguin or a seasoned Jedi Polar Bear, everyone is treated with equal respect and admiration for taking on the challenge, and the support and camaraderie from others is a big part of the enjoyment. Here, Patrick talks about how he joined in the challenge for his first year of winter swimming, and it has given him a love for cold water:

An orca's awakening.

To set the scene, in May 2021, my wife went on her first open-water swimming trip with our old neighbours to QuaySwim in Mytchett ... and they promptly did a 1k! They asked me if I would join them next time, to which they got the brusque retort of 'hell will freeze over' blah, blah, blah!

The following week, I joined them at the lake (albeit I cycled there) just to have a cup of tea; the same question was asked. This time, I pointed to the shortest loop and muttered something about the embarrassment that would come with being hitched out by the lifeguards, as I would not be able to circumnavigate it. Also, look at all those athletic triathletes, whereas I looked like a beached Beluga!

In mid-August, under duress, I entered the water, pasty-white and resplendent in neoprene shorts and a neoprene vest that rode up to the point that I looked like an overfilled Oreo biscuit. I set out hesitantly but was amazed by two things: the whaling fleet was not present in the lake, and I could swim 500 metres. The next morning, I managed 750 metres and the following session a kilometre. Blimey, I could actually do this, and now I was hooked … see the purchases of kit!

Open-water swimming is a very sociable pastime and people talk: 'Where do you swim?' 'Have you joined xxx Facebook group?' 'Are you doing the Polar Bear Challenge? … and if not you should'. Well, it would have been rude not to follow the suggestions.

Being naïve, we set our sights low – could we really swim a kilometre a month in winter? So, we (I roped my wife in, as it was all her fault after all) signed up for Penguin Gold with an added Polar Silver on the side (the latter was downgraded to Classic as my hands said no).

I soon realised I had short-changed us both, as individual ability, when coupled with the camaraderie of other slightly bonkers swimmers, means you can do a whole lot more than you think you can.

By the end of the challenge, we had smashed the distance requirements (over 100k and over 50k respectively), I had completed all of the swims for the Ninja level and managed distances that I never felt possible for somebody who 'WAS NOT A SWIMMER'. More than that, we had met some of the most delightful people you could wish to meet, all of whom are one boat short of a regatta yet have an inner being that makes them get into freezing cold waters in a variety of outfits, shriek and holler like banshees, and then calmly swim while the water eases their very souls.

I feel blessed to have been able to do this.

Next year, that Ninja badge is mine!

PATRICK LACEY

We occasionally get together in different corners of the country over the winter for a Gathering of Polar Bears and Penguins and that's where the friendships built online transform themselves into real-life interactions. Here, Barbara, a Penguin, talks about the impact that the challenge has had in forming friendships through the events:

January 2021

Facebook … what's this thing with people in wheelie bins full of water?! I'd fallen into the wonderful world of the Polar Bear Challenge. I've always dipped, but not regularly, during the winter. I didn't want to stop swimming in the Itchen once autumn arrived. It had taken me a year to get the courage to go back into the rivers; having got back at the end of July, I needed to calm my mind and outdoor swimming has always been my love. So on 12 September, I eagerly signed up! Best thing ever! I swim with Hampshire Open Water Swimmers; I'm a bobber! I love to swoosh with the current. I started putting up an event for a Tuesday morning swim, as I knew it would get me into the water, even if it was gloomy – and it did. I've laughed, sworn, giggled like a schoolgirl with other ladies in bobble hats, eaten cake in the car park standing in a bucket and introduced complete beginners to outdoor winter swimming, in February! It's been the best of experiences, and I can honestly say it's been the best winter ever. And I won a toy penguin for being fabulous from Pauline Barker herself during one of the meets! I'm hoping to be a Silver Penguin this year.

BARBARA COLSON

While the Polar Bear Challenge is not a charity event, a portion of the entry fees is donated to charity each year, and because the swimmers taking part are putting themselves through an arduous and demanding few months, they quite often use this as a means to raise money for charities and good causes close to their hearts. In each of the last two seasons, over £100,000 has been donated to charities.

WENDY, LISA AND JULIA

HAMPSHIRE OPEN WATER SWIMMERS

This chapter is in memory of Sophie Gill.
We will see you in the water.

The following short extracts are by some of the members of Hampshire Open Water Swimmers (HOWS). The stories have been patched together to give an insight into the place that swimming has in the lives of swimmers. The warmth of the friendship in the swimming communities is often the opposite of the cold that we feel in the water!

WENDY

I have always loved water and as a child it was my happy place. I was the girl with long hair in bunches and National Health glasses who was good at school, particularly maths, and was never part of the 'cool gang'. However, I was a really good swimmer, particularly the backstroke, where without my glasses I couldn't see where I was going, but neither could the other competitors. I swam for my county and my achievements were celebrated by people outside of my family, which felt good; the water was the one place I was 'cool'.

All the sports I have ever loved have been water-based. I was a wind-surfer in my teens, and in my early twenties I travelled around Australia for a year and learnt to scuba dive. I will never forget the way the water supported my body and the feeling of weightlessness – it is magical.

About four years ago, I booked a SwimTrek holiday and decided that I needed to get used to open-water swimming again, so I joined HOWS. The memory of meeting up with the group in the car park at Burridge and walking down to the Hamble, with a mix of fear and excitement in my belly, will stay with me. Swimming and chatting became therapeutic. I've read some of Clare Balding's books and listened to her interviews with people as they walk, and there is an ability to talk about stuff when travelling side by side that you would never do sitting facing someone over coffee.

I am in my mid-fifties and my body is changing. I am divorced, ten years ago, have always been career-focused and have held very senior roles. The menopause has made me anxious and doubt my ability. I am very aware that stuff I would have done without thinking about in the past now keeps me awake at night, but I push myself to do it anyway. Open-water swimming is my reference point: if I can swoosh down the Itchen for about a kilometre in water that is less than 5 °C, then I can do anything! I still feel that mix of fear and excitement before I get into the water, and my mantra of 'We do this for fun!' has caught on with others, along with 'Holy crap on a cracker!' as I get in the cold water.

Once in, the journey begins – literally as well as figuratively. The anxiety is washed away and I become me again. While I swim, there is time to think, at least when the water is warm enough – in winter, it is pretty much about concentrating on staying alive! I have time in the water to allow my mind to be creative: I mull over my garden and plants; plan meals for friends, artwork and designs; consider all the things I don't usually have space for. My confidence returns and all is right with my world. I don't know if there is a plug that the negative flows out through or a tap that fills up the positive, but my balance is corrected. The feeling after a swim is amazing – the endorphins race round my body as I drive home with the music turned up ear-splittingly loud; singing along is a feeling of pure joy. The water has literally washed away the self-doubt and I can achieve anything.

My swim tribe are part of my soul; like the water, they support me, protect me and envelop me. I have never met anyone swimming I didn't like, and I've met a select few I love beyond words. So, if you can't find me anytime, chances are I've gone swimming.

LISA

Well, that was an interesting river swim …

We were abused at the start of the swim by some teenage lads – just bad language, etc. When I asked them to stop, they of course just insulted us and swore more (although Heather told them what for), and then they decided they were going to swim down the river with us. They and I very quickly realised they could not make it and got themselves exhausted and in trouble, leading me to going back and us all looking after them. At one point, I had two on my tow float while I pulled them along and encouraged the other two to lie on their backs so they could keep going. I got chatting with them all and the bravado left. I explained about tides and currents and so on. When I said that maybe they should think about how they talk to people, as those people might be the ones who end up having to rescue them, one lad turned to the other gobby one and said, 'You should say sorry.' Maybe they'll think twice, who knows? I just hope they learnt some water safety and get swimming lessons.

These boys did not understand the community spirit that comes with wild swimming and the associated dangers of the sport, but I did, and although they were my abusers, I knew I still needed to show them the compassion and camaraderie of the community spirit of wild swimmers. I had the knowledge, strength and skill to aid them and also the maturity to put hurt pride aside – and I am grateful everyone was able to return safely to shore.

JULIA

It's Saturday 24 July 2021 and a beautiful sunny day. I'm packing my car with my swimming kit, along with bunting, a picnic blanket and some yummy food, as my swim buddies and I are meeting at one of our favourite spots for a swim in the sea, followed by a picnic to celebrate our lovely friend Rachel's 40.5th – yes, that's right: 40.5. Due to Covid restrictions at the end of January 2021, we weren't able to have our usual celebratory swim on Rachel's fortieth birthday, so we're having an 'official birthday' for her so we can get together and celebrate her and the lovely friendship we have by frolicking in the waves, dressing as mermaids and eating lots of cake. Twelve of us are meeting today, which is a luxury. Our little 'swim pod' formed in June 2020 when lockdown restrictions allowed us to meet in groups of six, and while we are all members of HOWS, like most others in the swimming community we formed a little break-out group (ours of women) to obey the government restrictions and help to keep each other and those we love safe. Rachel J., Rachel E., Wendy, Lisa, Jean, Lizzie, Alice and I formed the original pod and had a little chat group to arrange our meetups. We could never all get together, so the Rule of Six was always obeyed.

The pod grew as restrictions lifted and now, nine months later, we often swim in larger groups, but our pod has a special bond, formed in those dark days. I honestly could not imagine my life without these women.

The day was wonderful: we swam in a glittering sea, wearing flower crowns, headdresses and eco glitter; Rachel E. wore her wonderful blue mermaid wig; and the birthday girl herself sported her mermaid tail for a while. Swimming and this small community of women have been a strength in the past two years. We listen to each other's sorrows, offer advice and support, but the most we get from each other is laughter. We have grown to love each other; we are a swim family. Swimming outdoors has brought us together, and we all love it. Outdoor swimming – or wild swimming, as some call it – is a completely different experience from being indoors. Being in nature, under the sky, is like nothing else and every time is different; it soaks your cares away, and swimming with others who share the joy of it just adds to it. We swim in all weathers, at all times, getting up super early to meet at sunrise, in the darkness, to swim under a full moon, in sea, river and lake, sometimes driving for miles to a previously unvisited place in the depths of winter when the water is freezing. We question our sanity and chant: 'We do it because we love it, we do it because we love it.'

And, like the warmth and 'buzz' you feel after a cold-water swim, these women bring a glow to my life.

COLIN HILL
THE ANTISOCIAL SWIMMER

First, I saw the huge trophy being carried through the office; behind it was Steph, making the rounds around the sports team desks. Someone from the aquatics team steered her towards my desk. 'This is Colin, he's just started and he's working on the open-water event; this is Steph, she just won a swim race, she works on the cycling events.' Steph seemed to weigh me up and didn't seem too impressed. 'Do you wear a wetsuit?' were her first words to me. I stated that I didn't and I managed to slip into the conversation that I'd also swum the Channel; although still not too impressed, she did ask, 'Do you want to come to the Serps with me for a swim in the morning?' (To throw in a bit of context here, the 'Serps' is the Serpentine in Hyde Park.) It was 2011 and I was working as the Technical Operations Manager for the London Olympic Marathon Swimming event and, though I didn't know it at the time, I had just met my future wife, although it would take a lot of swims and some time before we actually started dating.

The next morning at 6.30 a.m., when it was still not quite light, I met Steph next to the Serpentine Cafe where the Serpentine Swim Club hut was also located. I was a bit nervous – judging by the size of the trophy she had in the office, she was obviously a good swimmer, so I'd have to bring my A-game. The Serpentine Swimming Club has been going for over 200 years in Hyde Park, central London. Club hours are 6–9.30 a.m., with swim races on various weekends. Steph was greeted by everyone as one of the family. There are a core number of regulars at the club; once the large number of triathletes tend to disappear for the winter, you are left with a group who turn up like clockwork each day. It was a mixed changing room, so being greeted by a naked seventy-year-old vigorously drying himself was pretty standard. Here, people look out for each other, have hot drinks ready and sometimes in the winter months have a bucket of warm water to stand in when you get out.

Steph introduced me to people in various stages of undress as the person looking after the Olympic swim event which was happening on their turf, so there were a few tough questions before I managed to escape from the warm changing room and into the green-tinged water for my first swim with Steph. The water was down to 9 °C and we were just in our swim cossies. I took a few deep breaths, adjusted my swim hat and checked my goggles, started my watch and I was off, head down and front-crawling fast to acclimatise myself. I noticed that Steph didn't join me and was happily standing up to her waist chatting to a few club members. On my way back down, I saw she had now set off doing head-up breaststroke in a woolly hat, chatting away to someone else with an even bigger hat with a bobble on the top.

Steph was wondering what I was doing ploughing up and down being a bit antisocial, and I was wondering why Steph was chatting while swimming breaststroke (with a dodgy screw-kick to boot). It turned out that, although there were some amazing long-distance and fast swimmers at the club, it was centred around the support group who looked after each other, and swimming was the catalyst for many fun swims combined with social events.

Perhaps up until this point, I was a rather antisocial swimmer. I grew up as a club swimmer; most of my youth was spent at the swimming club and swimming galas, until white-water kayaking took precedence, and I continued to race and train hard. I left the UK for nine years and became a white-water rafting guide, seeking out the world's biggest white water. I kept swimming whenever I had the chance, and that increased dramatically when I spent a couple of years in New Zealand. In Auckland, I was training seriously with a swim club again with plenty of sea swimming, swim/run events and adventure racing.

When I returned to the UK, I wanted to move back to the Lake District, where I had spent my gap year working at Ullswater as an outdoor instructor. I joined a swim club in Troutbeck (sadly, the swimming pool has now gone) who had a British Long Distance Swimming Association (BLDSA) enthusiast coach, Sue. I took part in the historic BLDSA Windermere swim race and went on to swim the length of other lakes there (and continue to do so to this day). My love of swimming in the Lake District was solidified. I didn't know any other speedy long-distance swimmers at the time from the Lake District, so my friend Dave would row a boat for me as I swam down lakes for my own challenges. I continued racing in triathlons and quadathlons (a triathlon with a kayak section), but I found that swimming was my real passion, plus I was picking up regular injuries from running.

It was when I was working for the Great Run company that I decided to swim the English Channel; it was a long time in coming, although at this point I'd swum the length of Windermere two ways a few times (twenty-one miles, the same distance as the Channel). Here is my confession: I love training, indoors or open water, so once I focused on the Channel as a goal, that was it. I was often in the pool twice a day and swimming in open water as often as I could. My passion for swimming spilled over into my work, and in 2007 I pitched an idea for a mass-participation swim with the same glitz and glamour as the Great North Run. As great as the BLDSA events were, I wanted to encourage swimmers who had only ever been in a pool to give open water a go. The first Great North Swim took place in 2008 with 2,200 swimmers, which was unprecedented for an open-water swim in the UK.

Around this time, I met Kate Rew from the Outdoor Swimming Society (OSS). Kate had run an OSS event in Windermere and it was good to get to know someone who was promoting swimming outdoors with such passion. There was a shift happening in open-water swimming, from the 'smothered in goose fat' image that people still had, to one where everyone would once again embrace the open water. I say 'once again' as there is an old, dog-eared book that sits on my desk. It was published in 1963 and is called *Modern Long Distance Swimming* by Gerald Forsberg. It talks about open-water swims and races as well as Channel swimming. There are chapters about the 'lure of long distances' and 'cold-water comfort', both of which appeal to my mindset immensely. Of course, swimming outdoors isn't new, but it has changed. Once, those who would call themselves 'open-water swimmers' or 'long-distance swimmers' were typically a group of hardy swimmers who would regularly test themselves swimming across channels or the lengths of lakes. Recreational open-water swimming tended to be at set locations such as lidos or at seaside huts. But now there are a huge number of ad hoc groups who meet up in random car parks next to various bodies of water all over the UK, with friends regularly popping down for a dip before work, as well as a multitude of events and swim challenges which welcome wetsuit and non-wetsuit swimmers alike. The odds are that many people at least know someone who likes to go for an outdoor swim.

Back in 2012, Steph and I were now officially dating and we were also swimming in the Thames at Hampton Court. Steph had been meeting friends to do full-moon swims for the past three years, and I was now part of the crowd that went in for a magical swim under the moon. We were also at the Serpentine every morning to swim with the now-familiar crowd of Serps Swim Club members. This was how I came to meet my next community of swimmers in Latvia.

Some members of the Serpentine Swimming Club were going to take part in the International Winter Swimming Association (IWSA) World Championships in Latvia. I had taken part in one of these before, in 2008 at Tooting Bec Lido in London. I was overambitious and entered every single race I could; I made a few finals but was so cold that I didn't take part in my favourite longer-distance event, the 450 metres.

In a time before dryrobes were a thing and before swimming in ice water was seen as a cure for most ailments, we headed off to Jūrmala in Latvia. The thing that struck me the most was that the other competitors could not have been any friendlier. The organisers seemed to spend time with everyone – Mariia (from Finland) and Alexandr (from Latvia) were obviously proud to welcome such an international crowd, with 1,000 swimmers taking part. An IWSA event is basically a swimming gala in water under 5 °C (it was 1 °C in Latvia). You can't dive in or tumble-turn, but otherwise, you have lane ropes and timekeepers. Some swimmers take it seriously and others just want to finish.

The feeling you get immediately after a cold-water swimming event is one of huge camaraderie, and I met Ram Barkai, who had just set up the Ice Mile, in the sauna after the swim. While still buzzing, I declared that I'd organise an event just like this and asked if he would like to fly over from South Africa to take part. Being an event organiser who was about to become unemployed once the Olympics were over, I knew that this was what I wanted: to move back to the Lake District and set up an international winter-swimming event. My name lends itself well to this (Colin Hill, aka Chill)! I set up Chillswim with my first event, the Big Chill Swim, an IWSA race with an ice-mile demonstration swim and talks from ice swimmers Jackie Cobell, Ram Barkai and Jack Bright. Mariia and Alexandr came across, along with plenty of Russians, Latvians and Finns. The locals, who were new to the sport of winter swimming, came along for the novelty, but were soon swept up with the international crowd obviously deeply committed to winter swimming. That's how it starts: one person goes to an event, goes back and tells someone else, then they decide to start winter swimming and tell someone else. The open-water swimming community continues to grow and grow.

Steph and I are settled at Ullswater in the Lake District with our daughter, Coraline, who enjoys open-water swimming. From my many years of being involved with all levels of outdoor swimming, I now spend each day, year-round, coaching and guiding swimmers of all abilities, both in wetsuit and skins (no wetsuit). I take swimmers out for their first open-water swimming experience, guide swimmers down the length of Ullswater, and host groups on night swims under a starlit sky. Hopefully, through my passion, I'm sharing the love for the open-water swimming community.

LOUISE OWEN
FRIENDS OLD AND NEW

You look down at the water at your feet, smoothly flowing or brightly lapping, still and dark or choppy and energetic, clear and crystalline or soft and soupy – it's different every time. Your landlubber self is appalled and aghast that you are here again, at the brink of an alien space, voluntarily choosing to throw common sense to the waves and enter this other, mysterious, icy world of unseen dangers and hostile intentions. But you are with your friends, and, like comrades bonded in battle, you step, stride or jump into the moment of contact, and you are all in it together.

On this day in May 2021, it was bright and freshly green and blue all around. The river was glittering in the late morning sunlight. The friends today were extra special. I'll call them H and S. We've known each other for over forty years, although strangely we didn't feel any older in ourselves in these circumstances. It was a sort of reunion. We'd met when we were eleven, at the start of secondary school, miles away in a different county and by a different river, but we were aware that lots of water had flowed under the bridge for each of us since we had last caught up.

Over the previous six months, I had found other swimming companions. I had extended my normal pattern – of sea-swimming in summertime, occasionally, when fine – and had embarked on a more deliberate determination to keep going beyond the 'sensible' seasonal window. I'd done some research (mainly from the legend that is Everyday Athlete Rach). Other people seemed to own some secret knowledge about safe swimming spots and knew of strange kit and preparations. At last, a friend in the know planned a quick trip to a local river, the Itchen at Bishopstoke, and showed me the ropes. Three of us hid our kit and hot drinks in bushes and I did my very first swoosh – pretty shocking, very chilly but utterly awesome ... and accompanied by great advice and inspiration! Soon afterwards, another group of friends were meeting for a fancy-dress Halloween dip at Test Marshes. That was obviously going to be the last swim of the year: it was windy, the water was cold and fast-flowing. I got out quickly and was very glad to be getting dressed and drinking soup – but what fun it was! At that point, I got in touch with one of these two old schoolfriends. H, who now lives in another nearby town by the sea, was also interested in continuing open-water swimming into the autumn and winter. Together we researched and explored and discovered the rivers and coastlines of our region over a long and diffi-cult winter. She was there that day, of course.

On this spring morning, there was so much more joy and hope and possibility and recovery in the air at last. We three had had the most beautiful fragrant walk through the bluebell woods of Bishopstoke and filled in many of the gaps since we had last met. All our swims, wherever we had decided to explore, had started like this: a good walk and a good chat. We all have grown-up children and shared their successes and concerns; we all had decisions to make about work and retirement; we were all to have the excruciating trauma of losing our mothers during 2020–2021. Negotiating the changing and baffling restrictions and fears of Covid had framed our lives. At last we were allowed to meet in more than pairs – it was now the era of the Rule of Six, and, as ever, open-water swimming offered its free, healthy, unrestricted adventures and joys. We had come out of a grim winter and felt like the teenagers we had been together, as if it were yesterday, as we set off up the tow path. The greenness was dazzling, wild flowers were in abundance and the bird-song was extremely loud (the airport remained quiet). The banks were also still quite unaffected by the larger numbers of swimmers who have subsequently discovered this wonderful resource, and we had this beau-tiful morning to ourselves.

We were so much better prepared than the first time – when we'd plodded barefoot up that stony path on a grey November day in our skimpy floral costumes looking 'very Torremolinos' compared to the bewildered, shivering, winter-coat-clad dog-walkers. Gloves, shoes, rash vests, tow floats, leggings, woolly hats, dryrobes and thermos were now all in evidence, and when we entered the water at the Second Dog Steps it was with that calm acceptance, recognition, familiarity and exhilaration rather than the shrieks, screams, operatic warblings, roars or colourful language that had accompanied our earlier cold swims! For one of us, S, this was a new experience, and, over the next few times we met – with another of the Old Gang at Meon Shore, or when we swam by the golden gorse bushes off Hamble Common – she opted sensibly for her wetsuit. But this time, we were all in a thin layer in the fresh, clear, chalky water.

As the water lapped achingly cold around our necks, we drifted down past the duck bush, the moorhen nest, round the bends, under the arch, past the rope swing, along the reed beds, near where later we'd be picking watercress, and the river bed rose and fell underneath us. Sometimes it's shallow enough to graze your knees, and other times you are out of your depth and swimming hard. And all the way, we talked and shared the beauty and reassured each other and marvelled at the phenomenon of cold-water immersion. We pointed out the pair of swans or the emerging insect life, anticipating the forthcoming season of butterflies and dragonflies; we wondered about the fish mocking us from below; and at times we just quietly glided suspended in a bubble of pure detachment.

I've swum here with other little groups of friends – the Funny Friends I used to share a weekly 'Synch or Swim' with, all through the darkest days of lockdown, off a boat way downstream, always more concerned with silly headgear and seasonal themes than the quality of the water or the very real worries we were often escaping. When we did that Itchen Swoosh, it was in high summer and we were surrounded by holiday kids swinging from ropes and hoping to save us from heart attacks! I also swam with the Lovely Local Ladies, whose real group name I can't repeat here, awesomely admirable hard-working wonder-women treating themselves to well-deserved escapes between important commitments, often with their families (and pets) willingly or unwillingly in tow. Book-club friends, random lovely people from Hampshire Open Water Swimmers (HOWS) and Kingfishers, all part of this community of swimmers … and I can't wait to bring my real hardcore ice-breaker Scottish swimmer cousins for a proper swoosh here when they come down to visit the Deep

South! Of course, this river isn't big enough for the full glory of the Southampton Bluetits, who converge in magnificent numbers on Calshot Beach almost as far as the eye can see and dispense much camaraderie and companionship! The open-water swimming community is as deep and wide and courageous and warm-hearted and fabulous as you could hope for.

The point suddenly comes when, instead of feeling refreshed, you feel uneasy, and usually before then you know it's time to get out. We had reached the First Dog Steps and knew this was enough. The final section through the trailing weeping-willow curtains is magically beguiling, but was not for us that day. We grabbed our coats and flasks and walked briskly back along the side of the wide playing fields to the cars, warmed by the sunshine and sheltered from the breeze. The next bit isn't always the best to tell people about, as it involves sticky, cold, wet swimming gear, ungainly wrangling with shapeless thick garments, chilly fingers and wrong decisions about whether to put socks on first or last. But suddenly you are enveloped in many layers from head to foot and gripping a warm mug ... and know that the fun is not yet over. For the feast is about to start!

As usual, H had made her world-class soup, different each time but always delicious, wholesome and warming, probably with foraged sea spinach and wild garlic and genius additions like roasted cauliflower and Thai spices. I might have made a cake full of fruit and seeds and good things; S probably brought salads, spreads, cheeses and relishes for the crackers. Whatever, we sat huddled on the grass, on the usual loud stripy blanket, and had our first summer-ish picnic of the season, as we warmed up and discussed at length the subject of food (in which we all take an interest!).

I had discovered it was difficult to capture the experience of swimming in a mere photo – the camera does lie! – and found that by doodling with a stylus on my phone (once I'd got home and was curled up with a cuppa), I could record my impressions so much more vividly. I could include the most memorable moments of each outing. And so the #swimdoodle was born, and I now have a large collection of digital pictures depicting almost all of the utterly different swims I have enjoyed with different friends and family members and groups, in all the many various locations and weather conditions. Gradually, people have asked for copies (the Kingfishers' Bat Swim at Moonrise was the first popular one!) and I have now turned them into cards and prints as @artylouimages. I was delighted to be showing these at the HOWS 'Toes in the Water' event by the River Itchen, and how wonderful it was to share in the creativity of these like-minded people. What is more, we managed to blend with another thriving and inclusive community, my musician friends of Southampton – and there was so much energy and joy in the room when the hearty singing of the HOWS swimmers met the epic Southampton Ukulele Jam and raised the roof of St Denys Boat Club! Both communities added to their numbers that day.

Our little group of three dear friends on that sparkling May morning represented in a microcosm the whole essence of this open-water swimming community, showing how finding people who will plunge into cold water with you multiplies by millions the many proven benefits of doing such a crazy thing in the first place!

SIMON HARMER

THE BENEFITS OF AN OUTDOOR SWIMMING COMMUNITY

When you see a bunch of walruses together, that's called a huddle; more than one shark, that's a shiver; and a group of beavers are known as a family.

In 2009 I received life-changing injuries; everything changed apart from my swimming. Both my legs were blown off in Afghanistan; after my initial recovery, I used swimming as an essential part of my rehabilitation.

Swimming has been such a massive part of my life; I have vivid memories of swimming as a child. Luckily, I took to swimming almost immediately; I swam most weekends with my friends.

I experience the same thing now as I did when I was a kid: excitement, unadulterated excitement.

Like most kids, I learnt to swim at my local swimming pool with my friends. Whether swimming with my school or going on a Saturday morning, it was always the same. My excitement used to grow before I even saw the water. It wasn't one thing; it was the whole experience. The build-up in arriving, my heart beating faster in anticipation. The chlorine smelling funny. The heat in the changing rooms as I jumped into my swimming shorts. Walking up to the water's edge and finally getting in. The feeling of getting in used to make me shiver with excitement, being enveloped by the water; it was exquisite. These sensations have never really left – I still get the same sense of anticipation before getting in the water, even now.

Much to my regret, I have never been a competitive swimmer; I didn't join a swimming club as a youngster. I would have enjoyed being part of a swimming club, I'm sure. It might have helped me develop my other swimming strokes – I never got the hang of the butterfly stroke; I can do breaststroke and backstroke, but I'm not that fast. Growing up, front crawl was always my favourite swimming stroke, and it still is, if I'm honest. And here's another thing: I can't tumble-turn. I think I managed a version before I was injured. But I certainly can't do it now. I'm now of the firm opinion that tumble-turning is cheating, which is why I probably prefer open-water swimming. Open water is a great leveller.

I still swim in my local indoor pool, more in the winter months, just to add some distance to my swimming. However, I don't find the community spirit present as much when I swim indoors; when I swim outside, we are all in it together, enjoying the fresh air and the open spaces.

Swimming was something that I enjoyed as part of being an able-bodied triathlete. However, most of my time was spent in a pool, and swimming outside took on a new significance.

I was injured on 26 October 2009 after activating an improvised explosive device while on operations in Afghanistan. After being rescued and receiving life-saving treatment, I was flown back to the UK for further surgery. I spent five weeks in Selly Oak Hospital; after being discharged, I found myself in Headley Court, the Defence Medical Rehabilitation Centre.

Headley Court is where any member of the UK Armed Forces can rehabilitate after anything from suffering a sprained ankle to becoming a triple amputee. While I was a patient there, I saw many injured men and women. My injuries were not considered severe; it was truly humbling.

Headley Court was a life-changing place: I relearnt to walk using prosthetic legs and took my first steps less than two months after being injured. The civilian and military staff were an incredible group of people; they changed people's lives.

I rehabilitated at Headley for four and a half years, but that didn't mean I stayed there all the time. Headley was a frenetic place; there were so many wounded men and women to treat and rehabilitate. I was supposed to visit in three-week cycles: three weeks at Headley, and three weeks at home. It never worked out that way. I had many more surgeries to endure, which often meant long post-surgery recovery.

My programme at Headley was busy. I had a mixture of physiother-apy, strength and conditioning, prosthetic care and swimming. Swim-ming became an essential part of my continued physical and mental recovery.

Not long after starting at Headley, a state-of-the-art swimming pool was built by Help for Heroes; this fantastic facility became a crucial part of my three-weekly admissions. After lunch, I would sneak up to the pool early to get in some extra laps; I was sometimes asked what I was doing there, and sometimes I was told I shouldn't go up early. That didn't stop me, though. I must have swum hundreds of lengths in that pool. That pool made such a difference for me; it changed my life.

Soon I was strong enough to try swimming outdoors. A group of patients and physiotherapists used to drive over to Heron Lake, near Staines in Surrey.

I remember my first session at Heron Lake – that sense of anticipation and excitement I had as a kid returned. Initially, I could only really manage one or two 1k loops; however, eventually, I got much stronger and faster. There was clearly a physical element to swimming, but I also found a physiological benefit from my swimming as well. Socially, I en-joyed meeting new people and making new friends. My mental health was profiting positively. It wasn't just the exercise; the swimmers' community made a huge difference to my ongoing recovery.

I have been swimming at Heron Lake for many years now. It is a bit of a trek from my home in Hampshire, but I try to swim there if I can. This lake has led to many life-changing opportunities and it's a joy to return when I can.

Over the years, I have swum in so many different places all over the United Kingdom. This sport has encouraged me to enter some incredible races too. Notably, I've swum Brownsea Island on three separate occa-sions; I completed the Dart 10k and the Windermere One Way, an event I have entered twice. Recently, I've swum Ullswater and Coniston Water. None of these events are particularly accessible, but that didn't stop me.

Why does outdoor swimming have such a positive impact on my mental and physical health? The physical part is easy to explain, but the mental aspect I've had to give some thought to over the years. The secret sauce is the community that goes with it – they make the difference. I am lucky enough to have an incredible group of swimmers I can call on.

Sometimes I might be up for a natter while I swim, or I might need a good training session; regardless, I know someone will join me in the water.

Recently, I found myself in a bit of a pickle. For whatever reason, I lost my mojo. Several things happened at once; it felt like I was overwhelmed and underwhelmed all at the same time. I couldn't function properly; I didn't reply to messages or answer emails. I could only manage the bare minimum, which isn't like me. My swimming suffered, which exacerbated the situation I found myself in. I wasn't in a good place at all. Apart from my fantastic family, the one constant I found in this mess was my outdoor-swimming community. They were there for me and made all the difference.

KATIE RICHARDS
COLD-WATER CONNECTION

On 19 November 2015, I received a text from my husband simply saying he wanted a divorce and wouldn't be coming home. It hit me like a tonne of bricks – so many questions, so many emotions. The divorce process was not simple, and it dragged on for nearly two years. It was all I could do during those two years to simply hold on, by a thread, by my finger-tips, by the skin of my teeth.

My priority was my son, a son who was dealing with the loss of his father, the loss of his home, the loss of his routine and security. Over time, it became apparent he couldn't cope with traditional schooling as well as his trauma and I took him out of school. I was responsible for everything: all the bills, all the decisions, his education, his emotional well-being, his processing of this situation. While I was giving everything I could to my child, the truth is that it was he who was giving everything to me. He was the strength and purpose that I needed to get through.

When we finally posted the keys back through the letterbox of our now repossessed home and crammed all the belongings we could into a vehicle to set out on the road back home to Cornwall, I was a broken woman. While I was going through the battle of divorce, I lost my job because I couldn't leave my son in childcare, and we said our last farewells to both my grandmothers, my great-aunt and several beloved pets. It felt like I was surrounded by loss and very little else. My son was a shadow of the laughing, happy child he had been. I felt that I had failed: failed at being a wife, failed at providing my child with happy childhood memories.

I was lucky enough that my parents were in a position to provide us with a home, but we were back in Cornwall, over 250 miles away from the life we had been building in Hertfordshire. We were reeling from loss and we were starting again.

Through the home-education community, I met an amazing lady, someone who while not actively in my life any longer will always have a special place in my heart. It was while I was walking across Porthtowan Beach with her one day that she took me to the Mermaid Pool. In spite of growing up on the north coast of Cornwall, my days as a child had been spent mostly inland with horses rather than on the coast, and I had no idea that this local gem even existed. It was a freezing cold winter day and we looked upon the pool and marvelled at the colour of the water. She turned to me and said, 'I'm going in.' She stripped to her underwear and lowered herself into the ice-cold water. With a few deep breaths, she pushed off across the pool and dunked her head underwater. She was in for less than ten minutes, but when she climbed across the rocks to exit the pool, she was a different woman from the one who had entered. It was as if I had witnessed the weight of her responsibility and worry lift from her. The complaints we had been making to each other about single parenthood and the difficulties of life had melted. She dried herself on her jumper and wrapped her hair in a T-shirt, then pulled on the rest of her clothes and we walked back across the beach.

Before we were at the car park, I had asked her to promise to take me with her next time. And so my first foray into what's known as open-water swimming, sea swimming, wild swimming or simply swimming was with this amazing and inspirational lady by my side.

My first few swims were scattered, once or twice a week – not regular, but whenever I could manage them. And I found that I could manage them, even as a lone parent. I could choose locations where my son was within sight and safe while I plunged, for sometimes just a few minutes. That evaporation of stress that I had witnessed in my friend became mine. For the short period of time I was walking into the water, all I could focus on was the cold, the water, my breathing. There was a break in my day, a pause, a full stop. The racing worry and fear about the future had to stop; there was no space for it alongside the focus on the here and now. And even if it stopped for just a few minutes, it gave me time to catch up with myself. It was space for my brain and my heart to just breathe.

As my confidence in the cold water grew and my appreciation for what it gave me intensified, I found I was raving about it to everyone I met. But the truth was that I didn't meet many people. As a self-employed single parent home-educating a socially anxious child, you don't get to meet many people!

And so I took my second plunge, this time not so much into water but into the unknown. I posted in a local female Facebook group about my new love of cold-water dipping and I invited others to join me. Hitting the return key was a scary moment. I had no idea if anyone would even respond, let alone brave the waters with me. It was January. It was cold. There were storms forecast. I was a stranger back in my home town. I wasn't the woman I had been before. I wasn't confident. I was scared. But I was also lonely. And I was hopeful that I wouldn't be alone, that I wouldn't be the only one who wanted the cold water but who perhaps also craved some companionship, some friendship, some community.

Over 100 women reached out to me from all around Cornwall. My mind was a little bit blown. I had hit a nerve. I wasn't the only one. There were women all around the county who wanted to take the step into cold water and didn't want to do it alone.

On 24 January at 10 a.m., under a grey sky soaked with Cornish mizzle, twenty-six women gathered on the slope to Towan Beach. Some were friends, but most were strangers to each other. All but a few were strangers to me; my friend travelled over fifty miles to share the morning and the swim with me, while my sister and her boyfriend looked on, camera in hand.

We headed on to the sand and found some rocks to the left, where slowly and tentatively, while questioning our sanity, we began to get ready; I looked around, slightly in awe of all these amazing women who had taken a chance on a stranger on the internet and rocked up in the rain for a swim in the Atlantic Ocean in January! The only common thread between many of us was the willingness to throw ourselves into salt water. We were women of all ages, all shapes, sizes and backgrounds; we were wives and mothers and divorcees and parents and sisters and artists and CEOs; we were locals, we were newcomers; we were just women on a beach being a little bit brave and a little bit wild; and we were taking time for ourselves, carving out a moment in our lives where we hoped to gain something.

As the minutes passed and clothes were slowly and reluctantly removed, the chatter increased, people stopped to stare, cameras were brought out by swimmers and spectators alike, encouragement was whispered. And then the laughter started. There is no sound quite like the laughter of a group of women standing in their swimmers on a windswept beach – if you've heard it, you will know. I've heard it. I'm pleased to say that now, all this time later, I have heard it an awful lot. That laughter – and it's a special kind of laughter – is the soundtrack to some of the happiest days of my life. But on that day, it was like hearing a new song on the radio. It makes you smile, it's catchy and, rather like the unexpected summer hit that has us singing along, before we know it, we can't help but join in.

The tide was out that day, making for a long walk down an exposed beach, with the sand holding the wet from the outgoing water. Our feet were cold before we even reached the sea, and still the laughter continued. I hung back and watched as an army of women walked ahead of me into the white water. I felt a lot of things that day. I felt relief that someone had actually turned up! I felt excitement, about heading into the water but also about the potential! Was this going to be a thing? Were we going to be friends? Were they going to love it? And, of course, I felt that break, that pause in my everyday single-parenting, post-divorce, home-educating, self-employed, housework-doing, lonely life.

We weren't in the water long. We splashed and laughed and dared each other to get deeper; we turned our backs as the waves broke against us; we jumped to try and keep our heads out of the spray; we held each other up; and we laughed. Oh, we laughed. That soundtrack on repeat. As we left the water, glowing with the lobster tan of a January swim, I looked around and all I saw were smiles. And still that soundtrack. Laughter.

To get in the sea on a winter's day takes courage. It takes mind over matter, when something inside you is telling you to stay on the sofa, to pour another cup of tea. When you arrive at the beach and the wind whips your ears, it takes courage to say, 'I'm going to take these warm layers off and head into the great wet coldness.' Walking out of the sea,

I often feel like the bravest version of myself. I did it. I didn't listen to the voices of comfort, I pushed myself. I did it. I achieved it. I won. I was courageous and I did it. And on that day in January, as I walked up the beach with these strangers, I heard their laughter and I felt their courage. You feel it and you see it. You see heads held high, you see women striding, the hands they had been using to try and cover their bodies up now being used to animatedly talk to other dippers. To feel happiness and courage and a sense of well-being is a wonderful thing; to feel that collectively is to feel it tenfold.

As we dressed, we lingered. No one was rushing to leave. Cups of tea were poured from flasks, hot-water bottles were hugged; people stood closer, their voices raised an octave or two from excitement and exhilaration. And I looked around and realised that, yep, this was going to be a thing, we were going to be friends – and, yep, they all absolutely loved it!

DEB PHILLIPS

CHANNEL SWIMMING

As my hand touched the sand, I tried to stand up in the cold, shallow water at Wissant, but my legs gave way. It was five to midnight and the beach was dark and deserted. There were no crowds to cheer or welcome me to France after my exhausting journey. I tried again and my legs just didn't have the strength to hold my body up. My friend and boat crew Ruth, who had swum the last 100 metres to shore with me, wasn't allowed to help me stand up – if she touched me before I had cleared the water, I'd be disqualified, even at this late stage. So I crawled the last few metres until my toes left the water and my whole body was on French land and clear of the Channel. Finally, I managed to stand up. I was shaky, cold and exhausted, but I was now able to have some much-needed support. It was hard to believe I'd achieved it. In this midnight hour, the boat that had supported me in my quest tooted its horn loudly, which signalled that I'd finished the swim and landed on French soil (sand!). After seventeen hours and twenty-three minutes of swimming, I'd become an English Channel swimmer.

The last four hours of swimming in the dark had been the hardest. As well as feeling fatigued mentally and physically, I felt extremely lonely and thought often about giving up. All my muscles ached and I'd had a pain in my forearm for most of the swim. I could no longer see anyone on the boat because of the lights on me, and my mind had begun to play tricks on me. Voices from within were telling me to 'just give up – the pain and cold will go away'. But I told the voices to go away, in much less polite language than that!

Years later, as I look back on the swim, I think the strength I drew upon to carry on during all the doubts I had has helped me with the many dramas life has thrown at me since. I've found an inner warrior woman I never knew was there. I've come through heartache, discovery of ten years of deceit, a divorce; but I found my true love and my life-saver, my faithful companion Sunny the cockapoo. I saw a phrase after-wards which spoke volumes to me:

'The devil whispered in my ear: "You're not strong enough to withstand the storm." Today, I whispered in the devil's ear: "I am the storm."'

I was forty-nine years young when I swam the English Channel. I've never really done anything as special and unique as this and I didn't realise at the time how much this adventure would change everything for me. Three years of training and sea swimming had become my life; I'd fallen head over heels in love with the sea. So, during my period of unrest, I decided to retrain and make this become a reality. After lots of intensive study, I finally became a swimming teacher and an open-water coach, and now have my own small business called The Sunny Mermaid (named in honour of my dog – I'm the would-be mermaid!). So far I've helped over 100 swimmers develop an effortless and efficient stroke and also formed many new wonderful friendships, as have my clients with The Sunny Mermaid Swimmers group.

I coach one-to-one from Lee-on-the-Solent, a beautiful part of the English coastline. The Solent is famous for its sailing as well as its wind, so coaching as I do from a kayak can certainly be interesting, although I only coach in weather that is safe to do so. On the calmer days, Sunny joins me on the kayak and brings smiles to my swimmers. When I first started sea swimming back in 2013, it was relatively unusual and the sea was mostly very quiet. Since the world has changed with all the lock-downs, open-water swimming has seen a huge increase in popularity. When the pools closed, swimmers had nowhere to go and found the lack of swimming – as well as all the news and the knock-on effect of Covid-19 – negatively affected their mental health, and thus many people embraced open-water swimming.

So what was once a relatively uncommon thing to do has seen tens of thousands of people discover the joys of open-water swimming – be it just dipping their toes for the first time to help their mental health or improve their physical health, or training for an event like a triathlon, lake- or sea-swim event or a Channel swim. I start swim courses with a video to show swimmers their technique and how it can be improved, and I always finish with a transformation video. Every time, the difference in the stroke is extraordinary. The Sunny Mermaid is helping them all.

This year, I have two soloists and another relay team training for a Channel swim. One swimmer is coming all the way from America to train with me and Sunny. I also have some non-swimmers choosing to learn to swim in the sea, which is such an important life skill and one very close to my heart. My father drowned in the Lake District when he was only fifty and I had just turned thirteen, which is possibly why I didn't start open-water swimming until I was forty-five. I'm so glad I did, though, as through it I've met some wonderfully inspiring, funny, creative and passionate people who I now call my friends.

STEFAN HARGRAVE
SEE YOU NEXT WEEK

The alarm goes off at 6 a.m. on a Saturday and I instantly think 'for goodness' sake'. At 6.05 the second alarm goes off. 'Fine, okay, I'm getting up.'

I stumble from my bed and creep downstairs, being careful not to wake anyone up. On arrival in the kitchen, a pile of clothes, prepped the night before, awaits me and I reach for the coffee machine to help the waking process.

It's dark outside and looks cold. I go to the front door to see if I need to allow five more minutes to defrost the car – luckily not this week. I wander back to my coffee and get dressed. I then prepare my flask of tea for later. Excitement over my new flask that keeps the tea hot – too hot really – is still there!

I head to the car, flask in hand, and I can hear the early morning hum of the world waking up. My swimming stuff lives in the boot of the car, which has the permanent look of having just been burgled! My car, and often the driver too, autopilots to where I'm headed, radio on and the rest of my coffee to hand.

As I pull into the car park, I look at the cars. I know who will be early, who will be late, who will step out of the car looking like a beauty queen and who will look like they had a heavy night.

Our little group formed during the early part of the pandemic, a group of people needing to take refuge in each other, as respite from being locked in, home schooling, the constant bad news. A shared love of doing something totally natural in swimming, yet a bit strange to most by continuing through the winter. This was accepted but rarely discussed, and each person leant on the group a bit more depending on what was happening in their world. The unspoken bond – formed through cold water, laughter and often bad language – got stronger each week.

We didn't know when we started meeting up just how important this little group would become. Initially we were acquaintances – we mainly knew each other through our kids' schools or sports teams. Now the friendships and bonds created through a love of the open water have seen holidays planned (with swimming, of course), multiple swimming events, day trips and, needless to say, the odd drink in a pub.

The impact on well-being and mental health probably can't be truly defined, as it is likely to mean different things to each of us, but the fact that we swim in all weathers, all temperatures and conditions and so early in the morning shows just how important this little paradise is to us all.

Our eclectic group, much like the Avengers without the weapons and the six-packs, includes:

- The Faffer – takes so long to get ready and can lose ten minutes because a watch strap is not quite correct.
- The Exhibitionist – normal changing protocols do not apply.
- Speedo Man – rocks the French campsite vibe.
- The Encyclopaedia Britannica – there is no event they haven't done.
- The Floater – can't wear neoprene shoes or topples over swimming.
- Jose – the special one! If there's an accident, it's Jose.
- The Unicorn – we know she's unique but we're not sure why.
- Jacques Cousteau – works in oceanography and gets frustrated that we still don't really understand tides and she likes to take the bait.
- The Influencer – the group photographer who does all our social media in the hope of being sponsored.

These roles are not mutually exclusive and most of the group will dip into the various roles within one swim!

As I get out of the car, a sea of normality, calm and happiness washes over me as the routine continues: 'Morning!' 'You're early, everything okay?' 'I had a couple last night, this is going to hurt!' 'Is Lucy coming; oh no, it's not ten past yet.' 'I can hear the handbrake turn, here comes Jane.'

We then turn to the pre-swim faff, chat about the last week, what's happened, what should have happened but didn't, basically all finding stories to delay the inevitable ... and at some point someone, normally the same person, says, 'Come on then, let's get this done.'

As one, everyone opens their car boot like a rubbish Red Arrows display. We then get changed and transform ourselves from looking like Bibendum (the Michelin Man) to a very low-rent version of *Baywatch* and strip down to our swimmers.

At this point nearly every week, a dog walker will stop and ask, 'Are you going swimming?' Depending on our mood, the answers range from a polite 'Yes' through to 'Nope, I just like hanging around in car parks in a pair of pants; would you like a cuddle?'

No one cares how they look as we traipse down to the water's edge. There are bums hanging out of swim bottoms and bellies over tow-float belts, but we giggle and watch the sun come up as we get to the water's edge.

It's January, the air is cold, and the adrenaline is starting to flow through our bodies. Without fail, as someone puts their foot in the water, they will say, 'It's cold; it's really cold.' We all repeat the phrase like a yoga mantra, knowing full well that of course it's cold!

We all march forward into the water like a middle-aged army until splinters in the group appear. The boob dippers go first. A quick drop into the water and then back up, as once the boobs are wet, they are good to go and they start swimming.

The second rounders then go; they don't want to be first but take great delight in not being last. Finally, the swearers – the ones who start by saying, 'for goodness' sake', 'this is ridiculous', 'why are we here?', and so on – get in.

Everyone is in, and there is lots of babbling, laughing and discussion about the water temperature. One swimmer will use his gentleman's thermometer to make an educated guess! Eventually, the call goes up: 'How long have we been in? Shall we get out?'

Immediately, 'yep', 'yep', 'sounds good', and we all traipse back up the slipway and towards our cars. Again, in one move, the boots open and silence comes over us as we enter our post-swim routine to quickly get as warm as we can in the way that each person has refined swim after swim. The silence is normally broken by laughter as one person gets stuck in a top, can't put their socks on or has realised they've forgotten an item of clothing.

Once the dryrobe army is ready and dressed, we grab our flasks and continue to chat about anything we can find. We know normal life is waiting, and we try and eke out the post-swim time as much as possible. Eventually, one person has to leave and so we all say our goodbyes and put our stuff away and go to get back into our cars.

'See you next week?'

'Yep, of course.'

SARA BARNES
THE GHOSTS OF COW POOL

Cow Pool is remote. Right at the head of the Ennerdale Valley in the western Lake District, further than most people care to walk, but not close enough to Black Sail Hut that people staying there might be wandering around. There is no tarmac road to it, just a forestry track, so you need to walk, mountain bike or ride a horse up there. Even on a summer Sunday, you will have it to yourself, apart from the creatures watching from the thick conifer forest that surrounds you. Discussions about reintroducing wolves to this part of the Lake District seem to have fizzled out, objections outweighing enthusiasm for the project. Belted Galloways roam free among the trees, mossy rocks, ferns and becks. I love the way they appear one by one, curious and timid at the same time. In the autumn, I have smelt them before I see them: the air here is a pure mix of cow poo and conifer with a hint of salt from the prevailing wind, which blows in from the Irish Sea across Ennerdale Water.

It can be a bit unnerving at the head of the valley – you feel alone, far from help, with no mobile signal and surrounded by towering trees, iconic crags and mountains beyond: Looking Stead, Pillar, Windgap Cove, Great Gable, High Man, Pillar Rock, Napes Needle, Scoat Fell, Steeple and Green Gable. A place of folklore, fearless mountain people and hardy Herdwick sheep.

A place to swim wild and free, whatever the weather.

Imagine a community of like-minded people, into hiking and wild swimming – what better place to meet for the day? Imagine the excitement of your first trip if you spend most of your time in a town or city, permanently connected. The novelty of leaving your phone in the glove compartment, leaving your car at Bowness Knott, a forest car park, and leaving your connection to anything but this, your own living, breathing community.

Lace up your walking boots, heave your rucksack on your shoulders, pull your hat down round your ears and let's go for a walk up to the head of the valley. Along the way, we can share our lives, conversation by conversation, broken only by the sound of someone calling out to get us all to crane our necks and look up at the sky to watch the buzzard gliding over the forest, or spin round to the left to catch a glimpse of a startled deer flashing its white bottom before running off into the undergrowth. We walk in a pattern of couplets, triplets and a straggler or two – the pace set by those more in need of a leg stretch or more desperate for the cold water we're here to surrender to.

We are fifteen strong – good company for those who want it, plenty of space for those who just want to be there and listen to human voices babbling like a gentle stream. Now and again, there is a burst of laughter or a squeal and the barriers of being strangers tumble around our dusty boots as one person recounts a joke or timely tale. I see Pete and Anna, a couple from Leeds who both work in the NHS, but whenever they have free time they drive up to the Lakes in their van and escape into the wild. Walking on his own at the back is Barry, who lost his wife a year or so ago and hates the sound of his own voice echoing around the walls of their family home. Ally, Heather and Lou only met this morning when they set off from Kendal in Lou's car, but already they've made plans to meet up again now they know each other. Graham and Olly sort of knew each other at university, so have a lot of old memories to catch up on; they set the pace, walking in time to the excitement at having common ground in a world that has fractured at its seams in so many ways.

I want to walk side by side with each person, hear who they are, believe in their dreams and weave our threads together into a colourful, evolving community of individuals who value integrity, personal growth, pushing ourselves out of our comfort zones, dipping our toes in the water of the unknown and holding each other up above the streams of disconnection and loneliness.

Who will find the pool first? Will they wait for the rest of the group to arrive or dip by themselves? How far does social responsibility stretch when temptation is placed before you?

We can hear it before we see it – water falling fast into water sounds like nothing else and fills you with a curious mix of fear and anticipation. I watch everyone's faces as we gather around the pool, body language telling me everything I need to know. This community has hiked eight miles along forestry tracks on a cool autumnal day, each person a beast of burden to layers of warm clothing, thermos flasks and slabs of cake. I can already sense the rich aroma of urgency and see fifteen bodies on the brink of shedding land-tied traits and transforming into aquatic creatures ready to slither and slide down moss-covered rocks, holding on to tough bracken stems and frondy ferns.

No signal, no green light, no bugle call: it's time to get what we came for.

Only none of this is real.

I am here on my own again: a grown woman with a bunch of imaginary friends. Rural isolation is prevalent, even in an outdoor adventure playground like the Lake District which draws people who share my enthusiasm for running, cycling, walking and wild swimming. Finding my tribe on my doorstep is a rare but exciting gift which has eluded me for most of the twenty-eight years I've been living here. Instead, I have found my tribe in the global soup of social media. Endorphin kicks, air kisses and emoji hugs are the currency of my friendships – priceless, but not enough to fill the black moments where you just want to share the scrapes and bruises acquired from scrambling down into a rushing beck, or try not to choke on an extra-spicy hot drink from the thermos.

Latterly, those online relationships and connections have been moving into my flesh-and-blood world, inhabiting my empty outbuildings and sweeping the cobwebs from the dusty beams. Late at night back-and-forth messages have become regular video chats and aeroplane tickets. It takes one strong link to hold secure until a chain is formed.

The cold-water swimming community was born online, but is maturing into something that flows between both worlds: there is a place for everyone, whether you want to bathe in the eddies, ride the rapids, surf salty waves or float silently downstream. Our combined knowledge and experience attracts new people and the chain becomes a multi-layered honeycomb of interactions and mutual respect and support.

So, on the rare occasions that I go to the Ennerdale Valley and walk or cycle almost as far up the head of the trail as I can possibly go, I always take my imaginary friends with me. As I stand beside Cow Pool, alone, I think of those people who would love to share this with me and I feel less isolated. One day, I will bring one or two of them here and another link in the chain will be created and held secure.

For now, though, I need to strip off and climb down the rocks above the little turquoise pool in Liza Beck until I am completely hidden from the track. All anyone will see are my clothes and a pair of leather walking boots, lying on the grassy patch near the little humpback bridge. My God, it's cold! But so wonderful! So many bubbles as the little beck rushes under the bridge straight from the mountains at the head of the valley – chattering like my teeth, frothing like the cappuccino I plan to order in the cafe in Cockermouth later. Bubbles go everywhere, out-of-control pillows of joy, no inhibition, no sense of trespass; they jostle and push each other, bounce off rocks, my thighs, my belly, my boobs and right into my mouth as, briefly, I duck right down under the water.

I've treated myself to a GoPro with waterproof housing and a floating handle. It's light, fits into my swim bag and I'm about to use it for the first time. What better place to baptise it? I have no idea what photos I am taking, but it takes my mind off the cold numbing my fingers and other bits. Glorious! The post-swim euphoria is tangible and the image of my face on my iPhone as I take a few selfies reflects my happiness and joy – in the twinkle in my eyes, the colour of my skin and the huge beam across my face.

Cow Pool: thank you for washing away self-doubt about my place in the world, reminding me that connection to others works in mysterious ways and connection to myself is the best possible place to start. You drew me into total immersion and reconnected my own spirit to the person I want to be.

The cold water has opened the door to a world beyond my tiny rural corner of Cumbria and the traffic flows both ways. Dipping my toes in the waves of a global communal ocean feels both real and surreal at the same time, but in those seconds where I've waded in up to my waist,

I know it is where I want to be. The transition from lifting my feet off the sandy bed and starting to swim gives me more pleasure than you can imagine. I soak up the warm sun on my face and relax into the ebb and flow of the waves.

If you are struggling to find your community, why not build your own through the things you enjoy doing? Like minds attract and language doesn't need to be a barrier to communication, especially if the conversation starts with a photograph of a sunrise swim or laughing under a waterfall.

You never know, maybe one day you will find yourself standing with fourteen other people around a tiny, turquoise pool at the head of a Lakeland valley. Then someone will slip on a mossy rock and land in the bubbles. You will pinch yourself and squeal, no longer there alone.

ENVIRONMENT

ALICE KLOKER

RIVER BED

One of my first memories is the word 'river'. I was reading out loud with Dad from *Frog and Toad Are Friends*. The book's author and illustrator, Arnold Lobel, was from the US, like me, but I can't help but think of Frog and Toad as English. In my mind, the book's palette of pale green, brown and sepia must have been inspired by the forests and chalk streams of Hampshire, where I've lived since 2013. We came to the chapter where they go for a swim. 'Toad and Frog went down to the RYEver,' I said. It didn't sound quite right. Dad unlocked the mystery of that word with his gentle correction.

Southern England is a relentlessly green place. My first and continuing impression of my adopted home is a place where green grows anywhere it pleases. Roofs. Walls. The pavement. On fences, railings, gates and headstones. Trees, grasses and hedgerows make their own green and also support even more green things. Vines, moss and lichens make their homes on bark, in branches and amongst the leaves of their host. River water-crowfoot and watercress green thrive in streams of flowing water, with lesser water-parsnip growing at the margins. The riverbanks are carpeted in yet more varieties of green.

The greatest reward for having endured my first winter of outdoor swimming in 2020–2021 was a heightened appreciation for summer. Gone were the protective neoprene socks and gloves I had donned after water temperatures started dipping into the single digits. I could take my time getting changed after I left the water, not worried that if I didn't strip and re-warm with enough speed, after-drop would hit me just at the moment when I needed steady hands to manage socks. Leaving the dryrobe, layers of thermal underwear and head torch at home, I was free to travel light and enjoy the extended sun of an evening swim.

My initial spring 2020 lockdown hobby was houseplants. I wanted as much green around me as window space afforded. I branched out beyond spider plants and Swedish ivy and made homes for peperomia, monstera, tradescantia and pilea peperomioides cuttings. I acquired a peace lily, and several fittonias in assorted colours. In my enthusiasm to see my new green babies thrive, I killed a jade plant with too much water. Sometimes, benign neglect is the best care.

After a month or two, I was satisfied that I had exhausted all reasonable indoor spaces for houseplants, and found I needed another hobby. I took to walking, and found that Southampton Common – just a few minutes from my doorstep – was home to a variety of side trails, side tracks and clearings deep off the paved pathways where crooked gravestones, ungovernable rivulets and mysterious circular structures made with fallen sticks could be found. I passed artists adding layers of spray paint to the brightly decorated subway under The Avenue, and found that if I just kept walking, I eventually arrived at the River Itchen, close to where it joins up with Southampton Water before reaching the Solent.

I loved walking on the Common. I still do. But as spring turned to summer, sweating away the days at my home office in the loft, I yearned for a new kind of outdoor experience. I worked up the courage to ask a friend who posted lush photos of her river swims online to take me with her sometime, if she didn't mind terribly. She was kind enough to text me one Sunday afternoon in August 2020, so I met her at the agreed spot, followed her up along the trail of the Itchen Way, walked into the river and floated along its gentle current to the exit point. I emerged happier than I could remember since the pandemic began.

My first swims in the dog days of late summer and early autumn 2020 were a strictly head-out-of-the-water affair. I had a passable if inelegant breaststroke, and found my side stroke worked well if I needed a bit of speed. I kept my glasses on so as to enjoy in the crispest of detail the scenery around me, savouring the overwhelming riot of green on the banks. At some point, the days got shorter and the water colder, but I kept on, adding neoprene socks, gloves and a woolly hat. I had my first swim in the snow, and marvelled at the transformation of the banks from green to brown, learning from my swimming community friends the importance of not touching the river bed with my feet so as not to disturb the trout and salmon eggs nestled in the gravel over the winter months.

By the spring of 2021, I had signed up for swimming lessons with an open-water instructor recommended to me by a work colleague who had also taken up outdoor swimming during the pandemic. I started a 'breaststroke to front crawl' course, and found it a much more challenging experience than I had anticipated. My teacher, an English Channel swimmer who accompanied her students in a kayak with her dog in tow, patiently taught me the basics of bilateral breathing and how keeping my swim cap on while I changed would help keep me warm.

I struggled at first with the sensation of drowning. Salt water poured up my nose and burnt down my throat as I attempted to put into practice her deceptively simple instructions to breathe in through my mouth and blow out through my nose. I wanted to gain confidence swimming in the open sea, so I diligently practised blowing out bubbles and turning my head to breathe in a shallow part of the Itchen. I practised a gentle stroke with relaxed legs, and after several lessons I found I was able to swim one, two and then three kilometres at a time along Lee-on-Solent beach, having found a new meditative practice that was not so different from walking.

Exactly a year and a day after my first lockdown swim in the Itchen, I went to the Lower Test to try out my front crawl up and down a tidal stretch of the river where, if you time it right, you can enjoy a good hour of slack water thanks to the Solent's double tide. I had gotten to know this part of the river well over the winter months, it being the closest swim spot to my home. As the tide rises, salt water flows into the river from the direction of Southampton Water and docks, and the current flows upriver. As the tide goes out, you can float down from the top. The swoosh is great fun in the summer months, but if you are going for a longer swim or a winter dip, the slack water at high tide makes for easy, dependable exit points where neither direction is too much of a struggle.

On one side of this part of the River Test is a nature reserve, an expanse of lowland meadow and pasture governed by several British environmental designations and one international treaty, the Ramsar

Convention on Wetlands of International Importance. Birding enthusiasts flock to the Lower Test Nature Reserve, where viewing screens allow the patient and lucky to witness sand martins, swallows and ospreys in the autumn; wigeons, teal and snipe in the winter; and, in the spring and summer months, birdsong from the reed, sedge and Cetti's warblers. Keep walking on this side of the river and you will come to a posh fly-fishing spot, owned by the Barker-Mill family since the sixteenth century. Ignore the pylons and high-rise housing complexes in view from the boardwalk which crosses the marsh, and you might forget you are on the edge of one of the world's busiest commercial ports.

You will soon remember, however, as you cross the railroad track to the other side of the river, where you come to the Test Valley Business Centre, nestled between Test Lane and the M271. This business park used to be part of the Barker-Mill Estates, but is now home to over a dozen companies, including industrial suppliers of everything from paper, computers and plumbing parts to heavy machinery. The centre also contains a few service garages for motorcycles, cars and commercial vehicles, as well as a chemical manufacturing business. Keep going up the road and you'll hit an industrial estate with an even wider range of businesses, including a fuel distribution company. On this side of the river, it's easy to forget how close you are to a Site of Special Scientific Interest containing one of the most extensive reed beds on the south coast, a brackish grassland with over 450 species of flowering plants recorded for the site as a whole.

On this early evening after work in late August 2021, I popped in my earplugs, stretched my swim cap over my tangled mane of lockdown hair and fitted my swim goggles over my eyes as I waded in at high tide to this salty part of the Test, the sun keeping my shoulders warm until I dunked under and waited a moment for my breathing to calm. The usually turbid water was clear that afternoon, and I could see right down to the river bed. I must have swum this stretch over two dozen times by that point, but I had never noticed the world contained on the bottom.

Flowing grasses, sand and silt with no rocks at first, then some – then many – rocks and different kinds of green. As I turned my head to breathe, I felt safe nestled between two lush reed beds blocking my view of everything but the sun. Further up the river, the right side of the bank was a blanket of pasture munched down by the Wildlife Trust cattle.

Continuing further still, the riverbank became a tangle of trees creating shade cover as the stream narrowed and my hands grazed against a carpet of river grasses. I kept going, exhilarated by the green above, beside and below me.

As happens when I swim, I lost track of time, so engrossed was I in the riverbed viewing, until I came to the final bend before the pedestrian bridge going into the nature reserve. The sight of bright yellow oil-absorbent booms abruptly terminated my swim-induced trance, and I stopped to tread water alongside what looked like giant sanitary pads floating before the bridge. I had almost forgotten about the ongoing diesel spill that had kept so many of us out of the Lower Test for much of that summer.

Sadly, rivers are not clean places after heavy rains. Agricultural run-off and raw sewage spills via storm overflows aren't a nice thing to put your face in. Swimmers know on such days to either find a controlled swimming environment or keep their heads above the water and hope for the best. In urban and industrial areas, a preponderance of pavement doesn't give the earth a chance to absorb the rains. Instead, it is all washed into combined sewer overflows designed to spill over into rivers, canals and the sea during heavy rainfall to prevent sewage from flooding homes and businesses.

In early May 2021, swimmers reported a rainbow shimmer of fuel oil coating the waters of the Lower Test at the bridge just below the drainage outfall for the entire industrial zone. It was much worse than normal. And it didn't seem to be going away. The Environment Agency was alerted, and later that month Southern Water vans became a regular presence in the upper part of the reserve. Despite the absorbent booms put in place and ongoing maintenance to the outfall, the oil kept coming back. By late June, images of dead fish and cygnets made their way into the news cycle, and unsurprisingly it was revealed that one of the businesses on the industrial estate was the culprit.

Each business on the estate is supposed to have a functioning interceptor to trap rainwater run-off from surfaces where oil is present. These interceptors are designed to stop contaminants such as diesel from industrial sites from entering outfalls – such as the one above the bridge – which drain directly into rivers during heavy rainfall. Businesses are responsible for having trained staff regularly clean their interceptors. The

Environment Agency recommends that they are cleared every six months, but does not have the resources to proactively monitor this. Funding for environmental protection has suffered under austerity, and successive governments have cut funding for the Environment Agency by over fifty per cent in the last decade. There simply aren't enough staff to deal with all of the threats to river health.

I stayed in the water staring at all of the padding designed to mitigate the fuel oil which continues to this day to leak into the Lower Test, and pondered the £90 million fine Southern Water had received that summer for illegally dumping billions of litres of raw sewage into our rivers and seas between 2010 and 2015. Two months after that swim, 265 Conservative MPs would defeat a proposal from the House of Lords that would have compelled private water companies to reduce discharges of raw sewage into British waters after heavy rains, citing that it was simply too expensive to make the upgrades required to our ageing Victorian sewage system in order to prevent such incidents.

Changes to our climate mean that extreme weather events are going to become much more of a regular occurrence in the coming years. Periods of heavy rainfall followed by periods of no rainfall are becoming the new normal. At the other end of this nature reserve are the Testwood Lakes, fed by the River Test to provide drinking water to Southampton and the Isle of Wight, which imports water in the summer months to keep up with the demands of the tourist season. I moved from my body to my head as I wondered how much profit Southern Water had made that quarter for its shareholders, and how many new Environment Agency staff that money could provide.

I then felt myself shiver, and snapped back into action as I made my way back down the river to the culvert, where a bag with my towel, clothes and water bottle sat on top of my clogs, waiting for me to return. I marvelled at the beauty of the river bed, and slid back into my bilateral breathing and focused on one stroke at a time as I propelled myself forward. The green seduced me back into my body. It wasn't yet 6 p.m., and the late August sun would be out for a while yet to warm me up.

After Frog and Toad go down to the river, it is revealed that Frog doesn't wear a bathing suit. Toad does; however, he is self-conscious about how he looks in it. He doesn't want Frog looking at him getting in or out of the water. Toad asks Frog to tell a turtle who approaches the riverbank to go away, but when Frog reveals to the turtle that this is because Toad thinks he looks funny in his bathing suit, the turtle not only decides to stay, but attracts a crowd of lizards, a snake, two dragonflies and a field mouse eager to be entertained. They all laugh at Toad's old-fashioned green-and-cream-striped sleeveless unitard as he finally exits the water, beaten by the cold. I wish I had one just like it.

SARAH SHREEVE
SEWAGE IN OUR SEAS

It was a gloriously sunny September afternoon – the sort of day when summer seems to be clinging on by its fingertips and the needling cold of winter swimming is a dim and distant memory. Earlier in the summer, I'd taken part in a study by Portsmouth University for people with long-term health conditions to explore sea swimming and its impact. As a result, I'd gained a ready-made group of swim buddies, and it was one of those friends I was meeting for this Saturday afternoon dip.

Sarah hadn't swum for a few weeks due to a flare-up, and we were keen to get in a last hurrah before autumn finally arrived. The water was like a millpond as we floated, chatted and made our way around the buoys demarcating the bathing zone. There was an odd scum floating on the water's surface, made more visible by the unusually still state of the sea, and it marred the sparkle and glisten of the water in the sunlight. I thought little of it at the time, and we got ourselves out, dry and into a nearby cafe for monster hot chocolates and more catching up.

It wasn't until I got home and checked my phone that I saw that the Environment Agency had designated an 'abnormal incident', and was warning people not to enter the water.

I was astonished, and immediately felt incredibly guilty for inviting Sarah into the sea. My mind started to race – what risk had I unwittingly put her at? What if something made her sick? I knew her immune issues were part of what had brought her to the swim course. I was also angry

80

with myself – I had prided myself on being well prepared to swim, checking tides, currents and wind direction, and packing my warm layers and hot drinks for afterwards. Naïve as it may be, despite a childhood spent climbing (and falling) in and out of boats in the Norfolk Broads and Scottish lochs, the issue of sewage in our waterways had never really entered my consciousness until that sunny Saturday afternoon. I took to social media, set up a protest, and six days, four press releases and many interviews later, 300 of us protested against the sewage discharges on a sunny, shingly Southsea beach. As it turned out, this was just the start.

My education into the many and varied things floating around in our waterways began. Initially, I focused on the obvious offenders. In our area, Southern Water had been fined £90 million the previous July for illegally discharging untreated sewage into rivers and the sea.

You may wonder why, currently, sewage is still (legally and illegally) being discharged. There are a multitude of factors conspiring together, leading to the toxic soup which so frequently seems to be pouring into our waterways.

We have a Victorian sewage system, which allows rainwater and household waste water to mix together under our streets before heading to the sewage treatment works. During storms, the increased amount of water leads to surges, which sewage works attempt to store in large concrete tanks, as the flow of water arriving vastly exceeds the speed at which the sewage works can treat it.

Two factors particularly affect this: firstly, global warming is leading to more rain (and more 'biblical' rainfall events); and secondly, our homes are now far more water-hungry than they were when our sewers were built. Washing machines, dishwashers, indoor bathrooms with showers, and hosepipes, hot tubs and garden pools are all leading to high water usage, all of which makes its way into the sewers and mixes with the sewage from our toilets, increasing the volume of water making its way to the sewage works.

When the storage tanks are full, sewage works are then legally allowed to divert the arriving storm flow (of rainwater, waste water and sewage) straight past the treatment works and into the watercourses, through CSOs (combined storm overflows).

This mixture floods diluted human waste into the marine environment, including bacteria, viruses, protozoa and fungi. Due to storms, these outflows are immediately diluted by the water they pump into, but some recreational water users anecdotally report ill health after swimming in waters after CSO discharges. Many other water users enjoy the sea or rivers all year round with no ill effects. As well as pathogens, the sewage may also increase the nutrient levels within water, which some suggest may lead to algal bloom after the initial discharge. This can cause disruption to the marine environment, and the flora and fauna within it. Seagrass and oyster beds are very vulnerable to this damage.

Human waste, and the pathogens within it, may be the most obvious issue within sewage discharges into our waterways; however, the picture is far more complex. Waste outflows also contain microplastics (from washing synthetic fibres, road run-off and litter), chemicals (from household cleaning products, washing machines and industry) and pharmaceuticals, including hormones from HRT and contraception, antidepressants and illegal drugs (all from human waste). Basically, if you put it down your sink, toilet or drain, it will end up at a sewage works. Currently, sewage works are not expected to filter microplastics out of sewage, or remove pharmaceuticals. They pass into our waterways, even in 'treated' water.

The impact of these substances on our environment is only just beginning to be explored. Microplastics have been shown to pass through the placenta, and have been found in lung tissue. Fish in Canadian lakes exposed to similar concentrations of antidepressants as those in sewage effluent lose their fear of predators. Trout caged downstream from sewage outflow show changes to their gonads due to the hormone levels in the water.

It has been my privilege to support the work of a local activist group, the Clean Harbours Partnership, as they have worked with scientists from Brunel and Portsmouth universities to explore these types of pollution further through a large citizen-science research project called Project Spotlight. Initial findings have revealed high levels of potentially harmful chemicals deriving from pharmaceuticals and recreational drugs.

The cost of digging up and replacing our sewers is huge, and the disruption (and carbon footprint) would be equally large. Pouring additional concrete storage tanks has a similarly large carbon cost, and many of our sewage works are in ecologically important areas or Sites of Special Scientific Interest. The lowest-carbon and least disruptive route to ending storm overflows, therefore, seems to be to reduce the amount of rain and water reaching the sewers, enabling the storm tanks to store only concentrated sewage, rather than the cocktail of rainwater, 'grey water' (water from baths, sinks and washing machines) and sewage. This work must be carried out at both a municipal and a personal level in order to have impact.

It's been a wild ride since that sunny September dip. It may surprise you to know that, despite all I have learned since then, I remain a committed open-water swimmer and have just swum through the winter, revelling in seeing the seasons come and go on the shoreline and the riverbank. As someone with a congenital musculoskeletal condition, I haven't found anything that compares to cold-water swimming for pain relief and supporting my mental health, so I have persevered and remained hale and healthy throughout my cold-water swimming escapades.

I do, however, find that my love of outdoor swimming has become inextricable from my drive to advocate for the incredible habitats I so love to visit. After a heavy rainfall, I can choose to stay on dry land, but the fish, plants and invertebrates of the Solent have no choice but to be exposed to whatever is in the outfall that day.

Rather than being disheartened, I feel compelled to fight for our blue spaces, and I hope that you do too. If you're looking for some impactful, simple steps that can help to mitigate your impact on our blue spaces, why not consider the following?

- Write to your MP and ask them to push for tighter legislation against sewage dumping, and to introduce legislation for better cleaning of effluent, to remove microplastics and other compounds as well as pathogens.
- Find and join your local protest group. You may even get some new swim buddies out of it.
- Think about what your household is putting into the sewers. Consider changing cleaning products for those that are less harmful to the marine environment. Only flush the 'three Ps': pee, poo and paper!

- Reduce the amount of water used in your home – add an empty plastic bottle to your toilet cistern to reduce water use, take showers not baths, and use dishwater to water plants.
- Consider installing a water butt. This is hugely impactful as it reduces the storm surges of rain into the sewers and also provides water for the garden.
- Keep permeable surfaces (e.g. grass) in place and consider replacing impermeable surfaces (e.g. by installing green roofs and permeable driveways).
- Take a mesh bag on swims and litter-pick as you swim. Fishing line, floats and litter all cause a huge risk to wildlife, as well as breaking down into microplastics.
- Use a microplastics catcher when doing washing, or install a microplastics filter on your washing machine.
- Join a local river or beach clean.

CHRIS THOMAS
365 SEA SWIM CHALLENGE

As co-founder of the 365 Sea Swim Challenge, my daily ventures from the shores of my home town, Brixham in Devon, have taken me on an unexpected journey of discovery. The initial invitation to swim in the sea so regularly was not something I had previously considered. This opportunity came at a time where I needed 'rewilding' and I accepted the offer, not without trepidation.

I have never been a strong swimmer and definitely not eager to jump into chilly water. I was not the first to get in the sea when we played around the coastline as kids, so I surprised myself in committing with a friend to embark on this new adventure of wild sea swimming, in all weathers, for 365 days, and setting up the 365 Sea Swim Challenge in 2019.

We started in July, when the waters were a reasonable temperature, thankfully, and soon moved into autumn and then winter, embracing all that the sea could throw at us. There were many days when the sea was rough and cold. The commitment to the challenge and the draw of the ocean kept us going through all the tough times.

Initially for us, it was very much on-the-surface swimming, nothing too intrepid or adventurous. That was until, out of curiosity, we introduced wearing a snorkel, dive mask and fins. This was the light-bulb moment for me. This dramatically changed the way I appreciated the marine environment by opening up a whole new world of underwater wonder.

We are not in the Maldives or the Great Barrier Reef – this is Brixham, where I have lived for the best part of fifty years. How had I missed all this wildlife? Sure, I knew marine life lived in the sea, but I had no idea of the abundance and variety of species so close to the shore. This really did blow my mind! In addition, it highlighted to me just how big a barrier the surface of the ocean is to so many people, hiding all its beauty beneath the waves. This was the moment my attention and motivation transformed into wanting to explore and document my underwater discoveries by creating a short daily video of whatever I encountered on any given day.

The realisation of how difficult it is to capture marine wildlife on film soon became very apparent. Everything moves – everything! – the water, seaweed, marine life, me, the camera. This was not going to be as straightforward as I had first thought. I would need to learn and develop new skills. Most importantly, I needed to consider how I, as a human, could interact better within this wild habitat and minimise the distur-bance created by my presence in this world. This was an alien environ-ment for me and very much home for the sensitive creatures that live there. Initially, wrasse were amongst the more plentiful species, with corkwing, goldsinny, cuckoo and the larger ballan wrasse amongst the most impressive in size. That said, the iridescent colourings and mark-ings on the smaller fish are simply stunning. My swim buddy, Duncan Kenny, and I were incredibly fortunate to witness and document a spider-crab moult event. This is where thousands of impressive spider crabs gather to moult their shells and, afterwards, mate. This was a momentous experience, not something I could have previously imagined witnessing within our favourite little cove. We learnt that grey seals are also regular visitors. These highly intelligent semi-aquatic marine mammals, perfectly evolved to suit their environment, are well known for their curiosity and, dare I say, playfulness at times. Having stared into the big black eyes of a curious 250-kilogram adult bull seal, you do appreciate their sentience and intelligence, while acknowledging your own vulnerabilities in the moment.

The interactions I was having with marine life dominated my thoughts. How were my choices and activities and the actions of other humans impacting our marine environment? What could I do personally to reduce any personal negative impact and influence others to consider this concept?

After observing lobsters and crabs reacting to my presence as I dive down to learn from them, free-diving surrounded by shoals of bass, seeing the incredible spider-crab event and experiencing seals nibbling at my fins, my attitude and empathy towards the creatures I have encountered has progressed. Being present amid wild marine life within its natural habitat has brought me closer to it. Witnessing at first hand animals simply living their lives and going about their daily existence, I have found a way to feel deeply connected. It is not just the creatures, though; the marine flora plays a huge part in the diversity of habitat which supports this underwater metropolis. I have learnt about and now support conservation projects on seagrass, and appreciate how critical it can be to the health of our planet, absorbing carbon thirty-five times faster than the rainforest, producing oxygen and supporting over a million species worldwide by providing a safe haven and nursery ground. I had no idea we had seagrass in Brixham; in fact, I had no clue that it even existed!

All these new experiences have had a profound positive impact on me. The development of the 365 Sea Swim Challenge community has led to new opportunities to discuss marine conservation and the marine environment locally, for which I am immensely grateful. Meeting new people who share a passion for the planet's marine life and habitats has taught me that there are many projects set up to help and protect these delicate ecosystems. I have also learnt that a little can make a significant difference. There is an abundance of energetic humans contributing to and gaining a better understanding of conservation. We are learning how we as individuals can have a valuable positive impact on wild spaces. I have been encouraged by how my videos and photography have influenced other people's personal journeys to be more mindful and to develop understanding of how they consider their individual impact on marine life and habitats around our coast.

LINDSEY COLE

THE MERMAID, THE OTTER AND
THE BIG POO

'Do you think it looks like a poo?' I asked my mum, before slipping into my mermaid tail.

'No, not really,' she replied, chuckling and shaking her head as she attached the brown, homemade, inflatable, let's call it 'thing' to the back of her canoe. The rain started to fall hard before I even began my quest to mermaid the Bristol Avon. I had eight kilometres of the Bristol Avon to swim on the first day. I'd reached Bradford-on-Avon before it started to get dark, by which time my paddling support crew – my mum and dog – were as wet as I was swimming. But I'd also come up with a plan to make the brown thing that they were towing more 'poo-like': a simple pair of eyes and a mouth, of course.

Britain's waterways have been in decline since 2011, putting wildlife at serious risk. Only fourteen per cent of rivers in England are considered to be in 'good ecological status', while not one of them is entirely free from chemical pollution, despite a target for all waters to be in good health by 2027. In 2020, there were 400,000 separate sewage pollution incidents, discharging for more than three million hours.

The Environment Agency's budget has been cut by seventy-five per cent in the last decade. It simply doesn't have enough resources to inspect and prosecute river polluters. So the polluters know they can continue dumping their waste into our waterways and get away with it.

Much of the river pollution comes from agricultural waste and raw sewage – so, in simple terms, poo. Aha, my homemade sculpture makes sense now, doesn't it?

Being an avid outdoor swimmer, mermaid and children's author, I wanted to raise awareness about this pooey problem and inspire children to help create some noise to protect their local rivers. Otters are top of the river food chain and are a sign of river health. Pollution kills off insects, which affects the fish; and if there's no fish for the otters, they'll say 'I'm otter here' and go elsewhere for food. So I thought a mermaid going on a quest for her otter friend would be a friendly way to talk to children about river pollution.

River pollution affects the entire ecosystem. And where do rivers end up? The sea! We must do all we can to control it before it's too late.

I'm not a first-time mermaid adventurer. In 2018, I swam the length of the non-tidal part of the River Thames – all 120 miles of it – as a mermaid, alongside a giant mermaid sculpture made from recycled plastic bottles, to raise awareness about the plastic pandemic. Along the way, I rescued a cow and ended up on page three of a national tabloid under the headline 'Mermaid Saves Drowning Cow'. A school contacted me six months later saying my tale had all the ingredients of a great kids' story and asked my permission to turn it into their school play. I went along to watch it, they pulled me up on stage, and lots of little mermaids and cows bombarded me with questions. It was adorable and inspired me to turn my story into a children's book, *The Mermaid and the Cow*. By reading my book to children, I discovered how much they love mermaids. They really do. I also observed that being a mermaid is a great way to talk to kids about important topics. So during the summer, when I discovered our rivers' health was struggling due to all types of poo, I thought it was time to pull out the mermaid tail again. And on this occasion, I'd be towing a giant poo sculpture.

I started my mermaid swim and poo mission in Melksham, which is actually not close to the source of the Bristol Avon. It's important to recce your entry and exit points on any swim adventure. I found it really hard in this instance to find a swimmable start point from the Bristol Avon's source in Acton Turnville, and learnt how the Avon is far less navigable compared to the River Thames. It has so many weirs. Traversing weirs in a mermaid tail would be hard enough, but while attempting to tow a poo?! Not only are weirs bad for mermaids and giant poo sculptures, they're actually not good for river health. They were built for historic reasons such as powering mills and redirecting watercourses. Today, they're mostly redundant and are left to make it difficult for fish to feed, breed and migrate; and they alter how natural rivers behave.

As I mermaided along my journey, I met experts and river users who told me their stories.

'Do you want poo in your river? Or do you not want poo in your river? Everyone at Warleigh Weir agrees: "No poo in the river, please!"' Johnny Palmer, a river activist, stated. It can't be made clearer than that really, can it? When Johnny wanted to find out why children were getting sick after swimming at Warleigh Weir, he discovered that his local sewage company was pumping raw sewage into the water, and that it was legal.

'So I thought we should do something about it. It's now activist time. We need to get attention from the people and the government to change those rules so they're not allowed to put poo in our rivers any more,' he said.

Further along the river, in Bath, Eddie, who lives on a narrowboat, often sees 'things' floating past his boat. 'I once pulled up an old bicycle while magnetic fishing and it was covered in wet wipes. It's disgusting.'

River guru and keen swimmer Michelle Walker, from The Rivers Trust, joined me for a swim on the edge of Bath. I asked her if we should just all give up on swimming in rivers if they are so filthy. 'If we make our rivers a no-go zone, no one's going to notice if the otters disappear and the wildlife isn't there. We must fight to protect it,' she said.

I became very ill after swimming through Bath. It had been raining heavily the previous day. Izzy Bishop from Earthwatch mentioned it was 'mucking season', so it was likely that all of the manure on farmers' fields was being washed into the river and this could have made me sick.

I pulled out of the water in Saltford, unable to continue that day. We used citizen science testing kits to check the water quality. Minutes later, our results showed high levels of nitrates and phosphates, which are both present in poo, soil and fertiliser. As well as being able to make us sick, when they get into a river in high doses, nitrates and phosphates can cause algal blooms. These algal blooms reduce light and oxygen levels under the water, eventually killing off plants, insects and fish ... which means no food for my otter mates.

'As the Environment Agency's budget has been cut, these citizen science tests are incredibly important and fill the gaps that the Environment Agency is unable to complete. Citizen science is invaluable,' Izzy said. It's also really fun, when you're not being sick.

On the final day of the journey, I was able to swim again and mermaided through to Bristol Harbour, where I was pulled out of the water by a group of outdoor-swimming synchronised dancers. They danced and sang around me as I gawped up, wondering what was going on. I had no idea they'd be there. Someone following my journey liked what I was doing because they love swimming in rivers and organised for them to surprise me. Isn't that wonderful?

There are so many people who care about our rivers and waterways. And we had seen them all come out in their droves in the last few weeks, raising their voices and protesting when our waters needed them.

On Monday 8 November 2021, a majority of MPs voted to approve a government proposal for the Environment Bill. It states that water firms are to make a 'progressive reduction' in dumping raw sewage into waterways.

I was disappointed, along with many others, as the move does not require water companies to take action quickly enough, allowing dumping to continue for years to come. There are no targets or timescales in the proposal.

The government's amendment replaced a proposal from the Duke of Wellington which would have placed a new legal duty on water companies to 'take all reasonable steps' to prevent any sewage discharges.

As Britain welcomed world leaders to Glasgow's COP26 in 2021 – a conference discussing what to do about this, erm, pooey climate situation – #StoolBritannia, #TurdReich and #TurdWorldCountry were all trending on social media.

However, we must remain optimistic. People are more aware of the poor health of our rivers than ever before. There are thousands of eyes wide open. We have better monitoring technology and active citizen scientists who will all be mobilised to hold the government and water companies to account. We must keep the pressure on.

I hope to keep the pressure on by taking *The Mermaid, the Otter and the Big Poo* film about my quest around schools and festivals, teaching citizen science and recruiting an army of river angels to help us end river pollution. Let's keep fighting and showing the love for our rivers and waters.

EMMA HARPER AKA MISCHIEF THE MERMAID

AIMING FOR AN IDEAL – THE GHOST HUNT

I sit with my face squashed in my hands as I speed through my mind, searching for the best swim adventure I could throw at you, the lovely reader.

This in itself is a bit of an epic, mainly due to the fact I only really find mental clarity after a proper Cornish brain freeze. There is also the fact I have dyslexia and ADHD, which lead to a fruity tap dance through the English language. However, here we are, so hold on tight, I am aiming for an ideal!

My name is Emma Harper and my alter ego is Mischief the Mermaid. Mischief is a mermaid who swims all around Cornwall raising money for children's mental health charities, visits local schools and nurseries to talk about ocean conservation ... and, still to my own disbelief on turning forty, has started working as an underwater model, which has even taken her to Mexico (I know, I can't believe it either).

Mischief is one of a small number of Certified SSI Ocean Mermaid Instructors based in the UK. She is working with Aquacity Freediving in Helston in Cornwall, opening up the world of mermaiding so you can have more fun, be safe and – for me most importantly – learn about ocean conservation. Mermaids have a duty of care to our waters.

When not being Mischief, I'm a mum of three and an artist, and have an unhealthy collective of health conditions, which have all helped me realise the vital impact of wild swimming on my health. Once you've dipped and kept dipping, and felt the results, there is no going back. Two of my children have autism, so the water has been forever a constant in our family's support and reset methods. There are thousands of tales about the physical and mental connections with the sea, but on this occasion I am going to tell you a different tale.

My little piece of this story for you runs more along the environmentalism side, and underlines how as a community we can truly be the voice of our waterways and oceans.

Every little whisper can motivate change, and when carried through wild-swim communities, even more so. When united, these mere whispers can turn into something quite powerful, let's hope powerful enough that change can begin to bloom and our children's oceans, rivers, lakes and lochs can still be there for them to have as a constant and a form of reset.

I swim and play-dive all over Cornwall. Being a trained freediver, I make sure I always go out with a buddy; I would recommend always pre-planning and knowing your buddy like the back of your own hand. We have a small swim family called MorSprites and Mermaids and we skin swim, snorkel, freedive, mermaid and GoPro play ... this is where we get creative with water and frocks, but that's another story.

One of our favourite beaches – in fact, I even had my fortieth birthday beach do there (lots of skinny dips, wahoo!) – is Maenporth in Falmouth. What a magical place, with wild-swim options! It has a mean rip current at low tide, so we always aim for a nice high tide, which also lets us have a wonderful distance swim out to the shipwreck situated on the left-hand side looking out from the beach. You can see the wreck from the headland above when walking from Swanpool to Maenporth. It gives an air of sorrow, as sadly three lives were lost there, a cold, heartfelt reminder that the sea is a great power that needs our respect. The *Ben Asdale* was a Scottish trawler that collided with the rocks in 1978.

To the right-hand side of the cove is an explosion of life, with fish and plants dancing around like a fairground. Nature's playground, I call it, free from the reminders of human interactions. We turn right to spy on the fish and swim in the cathedral-like sea caves and underwater swim-throughs, where the kelp waltz by your side. Either side of this cove provides an experience to cherish, but both are strangely quite different. On this one particular day, though, we chose left, out to the

Ben Asdale. The swell was up and visibility could have been better, but there was a team of us and we had made our plan. We were on a ghost hunt.

Kitted up with our dive knives, we made our way out to the ship-wreck. The sun kept slicing through the grey cloud cover like dramatic stage lighting. When it pushed through the water's surface into the teal, it seemed to expand even more. Bouncing in the water, we looked and hunted for our ghost. We had seen on a previous visit a large discarded fishing net which had become caught up on the shipwreck. We had reviewed the situation and decided that it wasn't deep enough to call in the big guns, aka the amazing charities such as (here in Cornwall) Fathoms Free, Ghostnetbusters, Clean Ocean Sailing and Sea Shepherd UK (happily I could list more). I would totally recommend reaching out to your own local groups for support and local knowledge. Ghost-net recovery is dangerous and should always be carried out with the greatest care. That day, our mission was to free the net to stop it causing any more damage to local marine life, water explorers like ourselves or marine craft.

The rusted copper of the wreck glowed through the teal blue like the flowing flames of a campfire. Added to that, the bolts of sun that cut through, painting themselves along this silent metal memorial, were simply stunning. We all looked down, silent, no giggles, no squeals, hypnotised by the beauty, remembering and contemplating the fear and the raw emotions the ship must have stirred up when she crashed.

The net was truly like a ghost swaying back and forth, gesturing to us – our ghost. She seemed to have entwined herself as best she could among the copper sculptures of the *Asdale.* With our knives, we worked to cut her free. It took three of us to control her. The swell had settled and the sky cleared, which made our mission a little easier. Once she was free, I worked with my friends to collect her up as best we could and attached her to my belt to drag her home. We had a respectful swim around the wreck, which still has its giant rigging and engine parts laid out at rest. We turned and headed back to the centre of the cove. Being the ocean lovers we are, we got distracted by swim-throughs and marine life as we swam. I struggled dragging my ghost and all the other items I'd collected in my belt bag: the sole of a shoe, the inner of a tyre, a can of Monster – there's always a can of Monster energy drink! Fish hooks and weights were all caught in the ghost net too, which I could feel against my thigh as I swam.

My smile felt heavy; my mind, as it always does, wandered, thinking of the animals who drag our waste around with them for a lifetime. All from the toxic soup we leave as our human footprint. The list of ocean conservation issues is totally overwhelming … and if I let the reality of it drown me each time I witness with my own eyes how we are destroying our waters, I think my heart could break. But what would that do; how is misery going to make change? We need communities of positive, motivated souls to help our industries find new ways to work and respect our seas, voices to remind us how spending our money is actually placing a vote on what we believe in.

I merely tickle the surface of what I can do to help this planet, but it eases my heart to know I am doing what I can. That day, we cleared bags of rubbish, a ghost and more: we cleared our minds and processed. We worked together, swam and made a change. Yes, another ghost will subsequently rise from its grave and cause more devastation, but not that one, not our ghost net (it's currently in my garden supporting my plants). Wild swimming has truly started me off on a journey of self-reflection, to the point where I've stepped away from it being about myself. Yes, self-care is important; however, personally for me, the joy comes from forgetting myself and immersing myself in my swim family, the elements and our adventures, which can bring me creative revelations, moral awakenings and, most of all, the warmth of kindness.

People are sometimes motivated to clean beaches, rivers or the countryside to make other people good. For them to comprehend the feeling of 'good', they need some kindness and community towards themselves also. So we need to not judge each other. I feel no rage towards the fishermen whose net we collected, nor to the child eating a tuna sandwich when you consider that sixteen fish died as bycatch for that one tuna. All I can do is try and shout out the truths, and may those who listen also shout out. Our whispers in the waves will get louder, communities will gather and shout for our world's waters. I wish shame on those who know the devastation their profit-making is creating. Mass industrial fishing is killing communities, and we can't take it any more. Our beaches are telling the stories of microplastics, marine entanglements, pollution from sewage companies making people poorly ... each year the process is speeding up.

The ideal – is it in fact a ghost hunt in itself? Can we come together and believe in ourselves enough to make a change? Water is empowering, soul-affirming, liberating ... it's even got a dyslexic writing this! Words hurt my head – placing them one after another is harder for me than for a mermaid learning to walk with one foot after the other. The thing is to try, always try. Always make the effort to remove the litter you see, offer help to someone if you see them beach cleaning. Read how your food has been produced. Learn and then educate – from my little experience in schools, there is no better reaction then the realisation of learning the truth, no matter how raw. Knowledge is power and everyone has the right to that power.

So, in the final part of my story, let me tell you about the ghost nets of this world, and how learning about the methods of fishing will help you make tiny changes that, when used as a community, could enable big changes. Fishing nets get discarded or abandoned out at sea, then they entangle marine creatures such as whales, sharks, dolphins and turtles. The weight of the dead marine life sinks these nets to the sea floor. Some stay caught there, continuing to trap marine life, and emitting plastic toxins that add to the plastic soup of the sea. Others feed off the dead carcasses and can get trapped themselves. As the tides move, the sea bed adjusts and currents move the nets. Some become free and slowly rise to the surface. The cycle can then all repeat, unless we intervene by removing these nets or starting to monitor and control their usage. Giant football-pitch-sized nets and bottom-trawling nets will only ever bring death and pollution. I could rant on with facts and figures till my fins fall off. But it's about wanting to know the truth yourself, and researching the facts for yourself. It's your world.

I swim in rivers, lochs and reservoirs, I swim in the sea. I swim the same waters as every single swimmer on this planet. Water connects us all and shares our stories, be they of joy or sorrow. It is our constant. We must love it and teach others why we love it. That's my ideal: no more ghosts, no more mysteries of where your fish and chips came from. Oh to be confident in humanity, that is the ideal ... Never say never.

SUSANNE MASTERS
TASTES OF WATER

Sweet like an unexpected kiss, a touch of fresh water on my mouth while swimming in the sea. I should have known from the swirling haze within the Aegean blue as I swam down towards the seabed that here fresh and salt water were mingling at a submarine fresh-water spring. Salt water has higher density than fresh water, so when light passes between them it bends, giving a blurry shimmer to underwater views.

At home in Bournemouth, a swim from my nearest piece of beach to the pier sets me longing for fresh water. Over 3.6 kilometres swimming, it's impossible to avoid tasting more salt water than my body wants. Days when waves make longer swims difficult still have a salty flavour, as inevitably I mistime breathing and taste waves instead of air. More recreational than dedicated in swimming, I've never experienced what marathon swimmers call 'salt mouth'. This long-distance sea-swimming affliction is not just a sore throat and mouth from exposure to salinity but sometimes also the loss of the top layer of flesh on the tongue and inside the throat.

Our bodies need sodium, which we mostly ingest as salt, to maintain functions such as balancing volumes of fluids within our bodies and to control nerve impulses. But drinking seawater introduces more salt than our bodies can tolerate. Our kidneys excrete excess salt in urine, but only at a level that is less salty than seawater. Drinking seawater dehydrates your body, as you need more water than you have drunk in order to get rid of the salt you've ingested. For us, fresh water is vital.

While we define seawater as salty, its salt comes from land. Rainwater and snowmelt feeding rivers and submarine springs are free of salts, yet water in the sea, which is replenished by rivers and submarine springs, is salty. As water flows through and over land, it dissolves and carries within it minerals from rocks. Water evaporates from the sea, leaving behind these minerals in the form of salt. Dissolved salts precipitate out of seawater and are deposited on the seabed at the same level at which lightly salted water is added to the sea. Overall, the saltiness of our seas is stable, although more concentrated than in fresh water.

Swimming in a bay in the Aegean Sea but tasting fresh water from a submarine spring is a phenomenon shaped by the surrounding geology. Karst limestone becomes worn with channels and tunnels that allow fresh water to flow through them. On land, this is seen as springs and rivers; when funnelled into and under the sea, these springs are more tasted than seen. In several seas, these submarine fresh-water springs were an important resource for ancient civilisations.

Strabo, a Greek geographer who lived from c.64 BC to c. AD 21, recorded natural resources and local customs in his writing. He described the collection of drinking water from a submarine spring in the Mediterranean near Aradus island, Syria. People used a leather tube and lead funnel to bring up fresh water, which was then transported to Latakia on the mainland. Mucianus, Roman governor in Syria in AD 67, also recorded that the island city of Aradus used fresh water from under the sea. This submarine spring supplying fresh water for Aradus and Latakia was a persistent feature, and it wasn't the only fresh-water spring under the sea that people used.

Both terrestrial and submarine springs fed by the Eocene Aquifer System supplied Bahrain, an archipelago in the Persian Gulf, with fresh water. Aquifers occur where water fills spaces within the structure of rocks. We see aquifer water emerge in the form of springs where saturated rock reaches the surface, and in some places we can access this fresh water by drilling deep. In conjunction with the surrounding sea, these springs also gave rise to Bahrain's name, derived from the Arabic *al-Bahrayn*, meaning 'two seas' – i.e. the two notable bodies of water present of fresh water and salt water. Fresh water was not just a practical resource for people; submarine springs had particular sacred significance. After visiting Bahrain in 1489, Ahmad ibn Mājid, an Arab navigator and scholar, wrote with wonder of a place 'where a man can dive into the salt sea with a skin and fill it with fresh water while he is submerged in the salt water'.

Bahrain can no longer rely on fresh-water springs for its drinking water supplies. Over time, Bahrain's underlying aquifer has diminished, and rainfall has not replenished as much water as has flowed out. The rain that filled the Eocene aquifer system fell 126,000 to 8,000 years ago. While this legacy of a damper climate is running out, human population demands on water resources have also increased. As fresh water retreats, salt water incursion creeps. Desalination has become a necessary means of supplying water in Bahrain.

Similarly, in Hampshire, aquifer water – here delivered by chalk streams – cannot keep flowing and catering to people's demand for tap water. Much of southern England's tap-water supplies come from the globally rare habitat of chalk streams; in the whole world, there are just 260 chalk streams, and 224 of them are in England.

Swimming in Florida's springs of crystal-clear water with turtles and manatees seems like lucid dreaming; you choose how to move through scenery that is too vividly turquoise and beautiful to be real. Extraction licences for bottling spring water are one of the frontiers at which conservationists and local people who just love their springs and the wildlife that inhabits them battle to protect Florida's springs. Although the Floridian aquifer that supplies the springs with water is vast, its output cannot withstand unlimited pressures of abstraction, and exporting Florida spring water in bottles is one of the drivers diminishing Florida's spring runs.

Alongside springs, surface water in the form of rivers, lakes, streams and reservoirs also offers fresh water for our needs. In Bahrain, southern England and Florida – and for most of the world's population – the problem of fresh water supply remains an issue, because clean, fresh water is in fact a rarity.

Water seems abundant when looking at maps and noting that seventy-one per cent of the Earth's surface is covered by water. But ninety-seven per cent of the Earth's water is salt water residing in our oceans and seas. Only three per cent of the Earth's water is fresh, and it is largely unavailable because most fresh water is solid, frozen in ice, gaseous in the atmosphere, or liquid but polluted. It's depressingly easy to pollute water. A gallon of paint or a quart of motor oil can seep into the earth and pollute 250,000 gallons of drinking water. One spilled gallon of gasoline can pollute 750,000 gallons of water. Of all the Earth's water, only 0.5 per cent is fresh water that we can drink.

Although fresh water doesn't taste as salty as seawater, it still contains more than pure water. Distilled water, just water molecules without dissolved minerals, tastes strange: wet but not quite right, in the way a savoury dish made without salt is odd to an unaccustomed tongue. We are used to water that is not solely composed of hydrogen and oxygen bonded as water molecules, but bears traces of landscapes it has flowed from and over in the form of minerals and sometimes organic matter.

On a Midsummer Day miles from the nearest roads, it was easy to hear the rippling pulse of a green hill in the Scottish Highlands. Rain caught by its slopes slowly moved through sphagnum moss. Boxes sunk in the ground pooled the soft creep of water into trickling flow, which was channelled into pipes. I was on fieldwork for a distillery that had taken me up in the hills to see the source of water they used at this spring.

In the morning I had gone for a run through the forest before breakfast. Several days of blazing sun had made the Highlands feel warm. Combined with running uphill, the siren song of a waterfall and invitation of a river pool were irresistible. Knowing that the previous night's product sampling meant there was zero chance of anyone I knew in the area being up and out in the forest, I left my clothes on rocks on the river's edge and enjoyed the dark embrace of tannic water.

While water flowing through upper levels of sphagnum bog on the hillsides took on no colour, water passing through deeper layers of peat picked up brown tannins from slowly decaying vegetation. In the gradient of shallow to deep, the river's water remained clear but segued from whisky- to coffee-coloured and, in the deepest part of the river pool, inky black. The soft, clear waters of Highland rivers lack the somewhat vegetal whisper of scent that familiar lowland rivers in southern England have. As much as Highland river swims differ from lowland swims in appearance, the aroma that clings to their water is also part of the contrast. How something tastes is an intersensory experience, as it is formed by both taste on the tongue and inhaled scent.

Whisky that has been distilled and matured in casks is about sixty per cent alcohol by volume (ABV). When bottled for sale, most alcohol is diluted with water from cask strength down to around forty per cent ABV. Water used in this stage of whisky production is considered to form part of the whisky's character. Though most distilleries use soft water, low in both dissolved minerals and pH, from springs in sphagnum bogs and sources on granite topography, a few, like Highland Park, use hard water that contains more dissolved minerals and has a higher pH.

It isn't just Scottish whisky that lays claim to the taste of water. Jack Daniels whiskey credits water from Cave Spring Hollow in Tennessee as part of the flavour. In addition to whiskey, the distillery has bottled and sold their spring water. Unopened 1980s-era half-gallon glass bottles of Jack Daniels limestone spring water are now sold online for more than the cost of a bottle of whiskey.

You can buy a gin made in England in which the full-strength distilled spirit is watered down to gin level of forty per cent ABV using water shipped in from a spring in Iceland. Its manufacturers cite the purity of Icelandic spring water as instrumental in shaping the taste of their gin.

It isn't only drinks that claim a role of water in taste; foods are also considered to be influenced by water used in making them. Running down from the Catskill Mountains, New York soft water that is low in calcium and magnesium is credited as the reason for New York bagels being superior to bagels made elsewhere. Calcium and magnesium fortify gluten, the protein in wheat that holds structure in cooked dough. New York's soft water leaves gluten unfortified and makes soft, chewy bagels. Although we pay it less attention, texture is part of the way we taste food. While Catskill Mountains water might be thought a gift from nature, the New York WaterMaker is a machine that replicates water from New York City and any other desired location by controlling levels of minerals in the water.

Bottling water and transporting it supersedes thoughts on what that water should be doing within the landscape it belongs to, and the huge environmental toll of shipping a heavy item. Mechanised water replication, and the dominant tang of chlorination in tap water, can also blur our sense of the landscapes waters come from. Swimming wild waters puts a person firmly in place. After all, while swimming, we both taste water we immerse in and are swallowed by it.

MENTAL HEALTH

CATHERINE WHITE
WAVES OF FREEDOM

Swimming for me tastes like freedom. It means leaving everything behind – my phone, my clothes, my protective outer shell, but also the trappings of my daily life. It means leaving behind work stress and personal crises. It means nothing more than taking a leap of faith, opening my arms to hope and jumping right in.

Swimming hasn't always tasted like freedom for me. This journey towards freedom has come in waves. I can still remember swimming for the first time. Little five-year-old me bouncing in my car seat, the sharp tang of chlorine as I entered our local leisure centre and the bright harsh lights and loud excited voices. I remember changing in the humid cubicles and taking extra care to walk not run as I made my way to the edge of the pool, even though everything in me wanted to run – to fly, even.

Fast-forward ten years or so and the place of my childhood jubilation was a prison for my teenage self. My freshly relaxed hair would be destroyed the moment water so much as touched it. And if I didn't wear it straight, then my swimming cap wouldn't fit over my afro. I couldn't win. There was no one I could ask for advice about this. The other girls had the sleek straight hair I burnt my scalp every six weeks to get. They wouldn't understand. I started hiding in the changing rooms, correctly making the gamble that my swimming teacher wouldn't follow up on my absence if I showed my face every once in a while.

Eventually, hating everything about the tight lanes, the tight swimming caps and the tightness of the space itself, I began to recognise that the brightness and the whiteness of the swimming pool made no space for me. So I stopped. And for almost the next decade, this was how things stayed. Swimming was not for me.

Then, in January 2020, as the earliest strains of coronavirus – at that time still nothing more than an unfamiliar word at the bottom of the weekly news cycle – began to ravage our world, my complicated, brilliant, deeply loved Uncle Delroy died without warning. It was so unexpected that when I found out all I could manage to mutter was: 'What? What? What?' I didn't understand. We had just been together at Christmas – ten days earlier. He'd seemed fine. We'd had an argument about Stormzy. I'd offered to make him an Aperol spritz and he'd said he was off the hard stuff. We'd done our annual Christmas quiz and he had been quizmaster. The only son out of seven siblings, he'd helmed our family since Granddad had died. So how could it be possible that he was no longer here? And, even more importantly, how could he already be gone when life had been so unkind to him? When he had suffered so much? Things were supposed to get better, they were supposed to work out eventually. But they don't always – and they didn't for him. I fell apart. My whole family did. And then, mere weeks later, the world followed suit. Death and loss and pain, unbearable pain, was all around us, everywhere we looked. I constantly searched over my shoulder, fearing it would happen again and reassuring myself that it couldn't. The worst had already come for me.

But then, in January 2021, as the third lockdown – the hardest one yet – hung insidiously over our lives, I received a text in our group WhatsApp chat apologising for the medium – and the message – and letting us know that our friend Simon had taken his own life. I couldn't even ask the question 'what?' this time. It was beyond all comprehension. I was silent. And somewhere deep, deep within me, I screamed. Inside I screamed for the minutes, hours and days that followed. But I was locked in my house, where I did not live alone and could not find peace, locked in my mind, which was knotted with the devastating anxiety of words that I understood on an intellectual level but could not believe to be true. And so I did not scream, as desperately as I wanted to, because I could not. I choked on my own sorrow and wondered how I would go on.

With no other option available to me in lockdown, I walked. Head-phones in, India Arie soothing the thick, choking feeling that consumed me. Right near my house was a lake. It looked mysterious and imposing, but I was drawn to it and kept going back there. Instead of raw pain, when I was by the water I felt something closer to a simple numbness – which was a comfort and a reprieve. It started to feel like a holy place. I was in awe of it, although I didn't know why. And then one day I decided to get in.

It was freezing. Really, really freezing. This was January – and I didn't have any fancy equipment. Just my bra and pants on that first day. I probably stayed in for less than a minute: just over to the buoy and back again. But, as I gasped at the cold and struggled to mobilise my arms and legs just like I'd been taught all those years ago – 'breaststroke, arms: scooping round for ice cream; legs: bend, round and snap together' – I realised that I had released *something*.

I became more proficient and adept, used to the temperature. As I started to swim more frequently and for longer, I began to shift the thick wedge that had lodged itself in my chest and my throat. It was as if each stroke, each splash, each gasp as I slid into the water loosened it a little. I started to feel freer, sometimes feeling waves of euphoria, even though that *thing* still gripped my throat like a vice. And then, after some weeks of this routine, it dislodged itself completely. My body still followed the same mechanical motions – 'bend, round and snap together; scooping up that ice-cream' – but I started to cry.

I knew from that precise moment that I would be okay. Even as my cry became a bigger and uglier sob and I started to choke, exiting the water to hold on to something so that I wouldn't fall apart, I knew that it marked something monumental. My swimming turned from being some-thing that I didn't quite understand, to being something that was anchoring me – keeping me. It became personal. It became political.

I became mental health first-aid trained and learnt about warning signs for those suffering from mental ill health. I became aware that men (and Black men in particular) are most at risk, but also that Black people are disproportionately represented in mental health institutions, more likely to encounter inpatient mental health services and be detained under the Mental Health Act than white people. I learnt that stopping swimming when I'd been good at it wasn't just teenage vanity or boredom – it was me being pushed out of a space where I didn't belong because nobody looked like me and had never thought to make space for anyone like me. I learnt that despite wild swimming being proven to boost dopamine levels and increase overall happiness, according to Swim England ninety-five per cent of Black adults and eighty per cent of Black children in England do not swim. One in four children leave primary school not knowing how to swim.

These facts both terrified and angered me. Being able to access that lake every day in the aftermath of my grief not only healed me, it saved me. Swimming should not be inaccessible to Black people or working-class people or any group at all. Desperate to do something about this, I started working with Soul Cap, the inclusive swimwear brand who are rewriting the rules around accessibility to swimming.

And somewhere along the way of doing all of this learning and grieving and swimming, I also started writing. I put pen to paper and wrote a film called *Fifty-Four Days*, following the journey of a girl who starts wild swimming every day for fifty-four days in the wake of losing her father to suicide. It looks at loss and how we grieve, but more importantly, it looks at hope – and how we heal. As well as teaming up with swimming and outdoor sport organisations Soul Cap, Seabirds and dryrobe, I also started working for PAPYRUS, the UK's young suicide prevention charity. I am so proud to have subsequently become an ambassador for them. Via *Fifty-Four Days*, I set the aim of creating new standards in mental health, well-being and inclusivity in the film and swimming worlds. I hired a dedicated mental health and well-being coordinator, something that is still not the norm in the film industry. We had open and honest conversations about our mental health. It was groundbreaking, liberating.

What I love more than anything about my journey as a swimmer is that somewhere along the way I found a community. I am now part of a WhatsApp group called Strawberries and Swimming, founded by a magnificent woman called Henrike who – you guessed it – has brought together a group of people who love both strawberries and swimming. We share hopeful and joyful messages, swims and experiences. We also rally together when times get hard – when a young man drowned in our local lake, or when a cyclist was tragically knocked down just cycling home. This for me represents the beauty of the swimming community. It is as much about the personal healing as it is the communities – families – we make along the way.

From Ella Foote at *Outdoor Swimmer* to Cath and Kath at Seabirds to Soul Cap's Michael and Toks and the entire dryrobe team, I have been honoured to meet and swim with a community of people who care passionately and are working towards inclusivity, representation and healing through the water. This is why I love swimming.

Coming back to my own journey – and my film – I would say that even though it tackles a subject as heartbreaking as suicide, *Fifty-Four Days* – and my own story as a swimmer – is about healing. It is about remembering and honouring those we have lost, knowing that there is no right or wrong way to grieve. It is about challenging the narrative that says Black people don't swim, and fighting for the little girls and their afros bounding into their swimming lessons on Saturday mornings. It is about checking in again on the older men who have lost their way and the friend that you're long overdue a catch-up with. It is about holding the people who are being choked by the thing inside their chest and the people who just want to embrace what life has to offer. It is about checking in on yourself.

It is for every single person who deserves to feel the freedom of the water and bask in its holy silence. It is yours. Jump in.

BETH FRENCH

THE GLACIER

Unloading my kit from the car, I felt odd, fraudulent, and like I had misread the invite to a fancy-dress party. It was July, 26 °C and I was in full snow gear: thermal base layer, snowboarding trousers and carrying an enormous bag stuffed with gloves, hat and flasks of hot drink. The bulky clothes hid a secret that I was relishing, like an illicit snippet of knowledge I was readying to unleash or a superpower cloaked by my meek and unassuming alter ego.

The car that had pulled up alongside us spewed forth happy hikers in shorts and T-shirts, slapping on sunscreen and brandishing water bottles glistening with condensation, icy cold, fresh from the cooler. Mutual smiles and knowing glances – or so they thought – passed between us. Most vehicles carried sun-seekers: families rewarding walks with ice creams, hardy hillwalkers hitting the heights on this gloriously sunny day – and the odd thrill-seeker hitting the snow slopes way up at the end of this alpine valley. One of the few permanent areas of snow runs, this glacial valley had something for everyone, from via ferrata to summer skiing, from hiking with breathtaking views to picnicking with the sound of cow bells tinkling in the background: a heady soundtrack to this pastoral bliss.

I was here for none of that.

I love the water – am drawn to it like a moth to a flame. The sea is my spiritual home, where the world makes sense to me. I had spent nigh on a decade exploring what was possible for my body to cope with in terms of endurance and recovery, swimming channels all over the world – island to island, country to country and continent to continent. I tackled swims I thought were close to impossible, stretched my own inner horizons by heading out into the big blue yonder, all to answer a near-life-long battle with ME and whether I was over it – was I able to manage my symptoms to cope with anything life threw at me?

Turns out I was searching for the wrong thing, in the end. The compulsion to push myself, to test my boundaries, was only ever going to end in a crash. How would I know if I had reached my limit until I broke? I discovered a more resonant answer to a question I didn't know I was asking: can I tell when I have had enough? Do I have the right to say enough is enough? Do I have the courage to listen to myself when everyone else might be encouraging me? I discovered my voice is as important as anyone – and indeed everyone – else's. I gave myself permission to stop – and it was marvellous. I became a better advocate for myself and for my autistic son in an instant. I have never regretted deciding to stop pushing, but my joy in adventure never waned.

But it did raise the question of what next? I turned to my partner in crime for inspiration: my son, who had been dragged into a world of adventure from a young age, who had never known a time when we weren't exploring somewhere, doing something. So I asked him what he would like to do – and he said, without hesitation, to stay in a yurt in Alaska, in the snow in winter … Be careful what you wish for! So we did. And while we were there, he, in all innocence, asked me if I had brought my swimming costume, because I like swimming, even in winter … to which I replied that I like my water liquid, thanks. So he told me my next adventure had to be to find a hole in the ice and get in the water. Half joke, half dare. I was all in.

Which hole? How much ice? And above all … why?! Swimming in the sea for pleasure, I need no excuse – it is reason in and of itself. It is boon and balm. On a calm day, it's a sanctuary. On a feisty day, a challenge. In any mood, it is solace and enriching, even just to be near it.

I am no stranger to cold-water swims – I don't live on the coast, so use a lake high up on Exmoor when I can't make it to the sea, particularly in the winter when the time to drive there is far greater than the time I might be able to immerse myself. And more often than not, it is too rough for swimming, so the lake gets used a lot. It also gets colder than the sea by a long way – down to 3 °C – and I am happy to wander in, bikini only, for a heads-up breaststroke natter with friends or, with hat and goggles donned, a more workmanlike front-crawl session.

But if I am honest, I never sought out icy waters. And, as far as Dylan was concerned, it had to be epic. It was purely by chance that I came across the Ice Palace – a series of 'natural' ice tunnels under and inside a glacier. The air temperature was stable and, to cap it all, at the end of a walking tour, the last tunnel had water at a constant 0.4 °C that the group traversed in a dinghy. But with special permission, health checks completed and waivers signed, you were able to dip – if you dared.

And the more I looked, the more I wanted to see, feel and experience. My *why* was becoming clear.

It felt all too easy to book, only a stone's throw really, in the heart of the Austrian Alps. I acclimatised in glacial meltwater streams – torrents of crystal-clear, bitingly cold water down in the valley, easy warming on the rocks at the water's edge. I felt like a nymph. The whole trip up to the glacier was surreal. Starting in the valley, we were basking in mid-twenties warmth, carrying cold-weather gear. The first gondola knocked 10 °C off the air temperature. Sudden, absolute, the layers started to go on. This is where the majority of families alight – for picnicking and gentle walks, restaurants and play areas.

The next gondola ride and another 10 °C colder. Hardier hikers and hardcore families headed out, most aiming downhill, the promise of warmth and cafes as a lure. But we still had two more rides to go. The penultimate stop is the ski grounds. Snowboarders mainly, most of the runs shut till the snows, but for the fun-lovers and thrill-seekers, a year-round piste and powder.

The final stop was at the summit and, on this day, startlingly clear and a balmy -2 °C. To be truthful, we felt overdressed. It is a tourist attraction and an incredible experience to go from 25 °C to -2 °C in twenty minutes of gorgeous-viewed gondola rides. And a picture-perfect pit stop for a summer holiday snapshot of a snowball fight in T-shirt and shorts. A toboggan run in sandals.

I was feeling steeled by more than the forethought of what was to come for my body: the rush of overwhelming sensation as I lowered myself into the water, the focus on relaxing – forcibly if necessary – as much of my body as I could, the absolute control over my breathing to ensure I exhaled completely to avoid hyperventilation ... the slowing, the quickening and finally the surrender as I gave myself up to this experience.

Yes, I was steeled by more than all that. I wanted to expose my frustration of it all – the human recklessness at our trammelling of the very nature of these delicate environments. This glacier – considered a success in glacial terms, as it is receding slower than might be expected – is not all that it seems. And I was preparing to go into the belly of the beast and go heart to heart with its core.

I was weighing up the niggle of whether I was a hypocrite, being saddened by the tourist draw of the masses while being there myself – and decided that, yes, I am human, and as is so famously noted, to err is human but to forgive, divine. And also, I had created a bit of a platform through my swimming, and I wanted to use it for good. I wanted to shine a light on the fragility of our precious planet and highlight our responsibility to look deeper than the filter on an Instagram post. The shockingly white snow, dazzling with diamond sparkles, the deep azure blue of the mountain air, wisps of cloud pouring serenely over a distant peak – it was picture-perfect and beguiling.

An international group assembled – some ten of us from four countries, all togged up and led by an experienced mountain guide. We descended along a trodden path in the snow to a grotto-like opening, innocuous and unprepossessing. Hard hats on, sunglasses off and in we filed.

The complete contrast was breathtaking in itself. Dim, coloured lights were sparingly used to reduce heat damage but allowed us to slowly follow our route, up and down, winding and wending our way through the very body of ice others were frolicking on above. Further and further in and down – the sheen of the ice tinged blue seemed iridescent and alive. It's hard to remember that glaciers are slow-moving ice rivers – very much alive – because they are so vast. And this one was no exception.

That is the stark truth of it: the mirage of stability from the outside was just that. This awe-inspiring slab was not receding up the mountain as predicted, but here we were, traipsing through hollowed and dripping empty arteries of proof that this river was losing its life blood from the inside out. I was affected as deeply as these tunnels were taking us – both invigorated and melancholy by turns. Childlike wonder at every fresh view, inciting ooohs and aaahs from this chain of global penitents. It was more of a cathedral than a palace to me. Mostly there was reverent hush in these hallowed halls.

Nearing the end of our hike through the mountainside, we came to a perfectly cylindrical horizontal shaft of tunnel maybe eight feet across with gin-clear water in the lower third stretching into the gloom. This was what I had come for.

The other members of the group gasped and clutched their coats close about them as I quietly nodded to the guide, set down my bag and slipped off layer after layer of clothing, my son almost uncontrollably squirming in anticipation and glee at knowing what was happening until I stood, deferentially subdued, in nothing but a bikini with swim hat and goggles tentatively in hand, my kit laid out ready for quick and easy rewarming.

It was all I could do to stop myself from freezing mentally. The enormity of what I was about to do hit not just me but many members of the group who elected to stay and watch my baptism in the ice. Slowing my breathing, centring myself, I stepped forward, towards a little wooden ladder leading down into the water. That first initial test up the ankle – a subtle swish with a foot – I felt the acid lick of cold pierce my being. Stay calm, stay focused and experience everything to the fullest. The guide helpfully told the congregation that the crevasse was sixty feet deep, but that a shelf of ice allowed me to step down into waist-deep water.

And then I was enrapt in the silence of sensation taking over – the thrum of the rush of blood; the guttural, bestial murmur of the last vestiges of air leaving my lungs, ragged and raw – as I pushed away from the ladder to float on my back, letting the staggering bewilderment recede as my body churned into action. My mind – so strong and often my greatest critic – in that moment was totally harnessed and wrestling with my body's natural response to fight the cold in order to make it my ally. Meeting eyes with the guide, another brief nod and I turned over, dropped my goggles into place and smoothly started stroking out into the water, into the tunnel and into the dark.

It was glorious – and bittersweet. I felt triumphant that my body was not just coping, but I could feel my internal furnace firing on all cylinders, frantically working to keep life and limb afloat. But in this crucible of human experience, I knew I would not be shouting from the rafters and could not in all conscience use this experience as a call to arms. It was too accessible, too close to home – too easy, even – to get to. I knew in my heart of hearts that this soul-searing knowledge of how perilous the future of this enchanting monolith truly is would be borne by me deep in my marrow, as the cold now chilled me. I knew that the beauty of any pictures would drown out the chorus of well-meaning words, however much I tried, and would further threaten the very sanctity and safety I wanted to preserve.

And I admit, I shed a solitary tear, deep in the bosom of the mountain, protected from freezing by my goggles, held close to me by the same – another secret to bear, one I was equally fit to bursting with, but one that I cherish close and only give full voice to up close and personal – as raw as my numb fingers that reached for the ladder once more. This is a precious place, and I hope you never go there. Take it from me – you'd love it.

DR HEATHER MASSEY

MY LIFE THROUGH OUTDOOR SWIMMING

My brother and I were let loose in open water from a very young age, following lots of lessons in one of our local pools. My dad was a keen dinghy sailor in his younger days. We spent a lot of time on a local canal learning to jibe and tack on his fourteen-foot wooden boat. We had to do this very quickly, as the canal wasn't very wide! On occasion, this meant that at least one of the three of us (but usually all of us) would end up in the water. We also used to regularly visit the North Wales beaches with our boat. We spent a lot of time having fun in and around water, all the time learning about the tides and currents, as well as how to avoid the many hazards the sea can throw at you.

My brother and I didn't make the best crew. We preferred to be messing about in the water, rather than on the boat. But what it has left us both with, is knowing to respect the water. While my mother and her friends would look after us on the beach, we'd be having our own mini-adventures and spent so long in the water that sometimes the only way to get us out would be to entice us out with food, drinks or an ice cream.

As an older teenager and into my early twenties, when it wasn't cool to go on holiday with your mum and dad, I had a brief dalliance with playing team sports – rugby, football, hockey. I wasn't particularly good at any, but managed to find myself at the bottom of every ruck, in the middle of every maul, and played as a hockey goalkeeper wearing all those pads. So, understandably, I had a fair few injuries to deal with.

118

A lot of time was spent rehabilitating, and I would do this in the swimming pool. So, even when I wasn't swimming for fun, I was still swimming to keep fit and be active in preparation for my return to the pitch. Finally, I reached the point where I was spending more time in the pool rehabilitating than I was playing sports. It was time to retire from team sports and actually go back into swimming.

Since frequently visiting North Wales as a child, coastal areas have had a strong draw for me. I was lucky to be able to move to the South Coast for work as well as study. In the course of my work, I met some pretty influential people who really altered the direction of both my career and the type of swimmer I was. This all took place in the early noughties, when sea swimming wasn't so popular. Dog walkers would regularly pass us scrambling to put on a dry pair of knickers wrapped in a towel on a blustery day, while also trying to maintain a little modesty. I don't think we ever achieved it! In the summer, we'd spend our lunch hours on the beach, frolicking about in the water before returning to the office to carry on with the rest of our day. Our office was only a stone's throw from the beach, and we all felt blessed to have such amazing access.

It was during the course of my job that we were working with a group of swimmers from the Serpentine in London who were all solo Channel swimmers. They were a really great bunch of people and I was absolutely awestruck by them. I'd swim in the sea and I knew how cold it was, even in the summer, and they seemed to enjoy it and thrive in that environment. One lunchtime, they asked me where the best local swimming locations were, so I took them down to the beach and we swam together. They were much quicker than me, but for some reason they saw that I was prepared to get in and give it a go and they really encouraged me to carry on swimming outdoors. They introduced me to local long-distance swimmers. Although I didn't have their endurance or tolerance of the cold, they were great fun to be with.

I went on to support a local swimmer (Anna Wardley) during her training to swim the English Channel, and carried on supporting her with what I thought at the time were crazy ideas to swim in exotic and not-so-exotic places. But I saw that she was motivated, focused, full of energy and had a great way of bringing a support team with her. She also raised a heck of a lot of money for charity. With her and through her,

I met lots of new swimmers and we would regularly meet up for swims. We started to think about entering events like the pier-to-pier swims and trying to push ourselves to longer swims or colder swims, before eventually swimming all the way through the winter months.

Although it's fun swimming outdoors, we couldn't swim for very long in the winter. In order to stay fit and have the necessary endurance for the summer season, I needed to train regularly, so I joined my local masters swimming club. It was pretty daunting joining the masters sessions, as they were all so much faster than me. But I hung in there and met the people who would later support me for my solo Channel swim. My technique started to improve, both in the pool and outdoors, and it felt good to be able to glide through the water with less effort.

I started enjoying it again – beasting myself in the pool was paying off, and I was swimming quicker in the pool and open water. I really felt that outdoor swimming was my second sporting career rather than a fad. It provides great friendship and camaraderie, similar to my experiences playing rugby. Rough conditions had always been a challenge, but I started to handle these conditions better (by 'better', I mean that I didn't take on quite so much seawater and could relax more), the back strap and hat tan lines became a feature, and I started to join in longer swims, including swimming the length of Windermere. The latter involved dragging my dad and then new boyfriend (now husband) up there to sit in a cold, wet rowing boat for hours on end supporting me during the swim. I could spend all day talking about this event and the steep learning curve we all experienced that day.

Other events followed in quick succession: the Guildford 2swim4life events, swimathons, Round Jersey, Jersey to France and Channel relays. I still look back and see the people that I met throughout this time – Anna, Chris Pitman, Wendy Trehiou, Sakura and Nick Adams – with great admiration. They had either attempted to or swum the *whole of* the English Channel, starting near Dover and finishing near the Cap Gris-Nez in France. Despite all of the events I had completed, I still thought that's not something within my grasp.

It was, and is, fair to say that the word 'IMPOSTER' was and is tattooed to the inside of my eyelids. *Every* time I blinked, I could see that word. I wasn't capable of swimming from England to France. Those words are still visible – although with age and experience they are fading, they still make a reappearance every now and then. So, what changed? Well, some of the friends I'd started outdoor swimming with were booking Channel swims. I trained with them, crewed for them, helped to feed them during the crossing and looked after them. I saw how they coped, and learnt what they did to prepare themselves. This process really helped me to learn about the craft and believe, but I still hadn't the guts to contact a pilot and book a slot for myself. It took one of my really good friends (Chris Pitman) to book the slot for me and tell me that I was swimming the Channel ... and that there was no point in arguing as I needed to get on and train for it!

Although I was reticent to start with, I felt I had little choice but to crack on. I'd seen and supported others with their goals and just needed to get myself prepared. I swore my swimming friends and training buddies to secrecy about the 'attempt', even asking the doctor who signed my medical forms not to talk to other people about me swimming a solo. I really only 'came out' about my attempt when I booked a training week in Croatia. But most people, including my colleagues at work, didn't know until I went to Dover for the first time that I was about to attempt a Channel solo. We'd put the obligatory Facebook notice out to say I would be swimming, the pilot boat name, how we could be tracked and what time we would leave – only within minutes of sending the message to be turned back with me greased up and ready to get in the water. The waves were too big and the weather forecast had changed. So we had to all go back home, watch and wait for another opportunity.

That opportunity came two and half weeks later. We were all a bag of nerves. Would I be able to get in the water at all?

After an eventful trip to Dover, my memories of the swim are fairly limited. Time seemed to collapse and I was just enjoying being in the water. I only really remember several key moments. The first was when I must have bashed my arm against something pretty hard in the water and had a searing pain going from my wrist through to my elbow during every right-arm pull for the remainder of the trip. Another key part was really trying to battle the imposter moments, the devil that was sitting on my shoulder telling me that I couldn't do it. I was tired. From the many training swims, I had taught myself to externalise negative thoughts. I'd imagine a rope around my waist and somebody pulling me towards France. And when I felt tired, it wasn't me that was tired, it was the person on the other end of the rope. And it was time for them to get off the rope and let another member of my team start pulling. In my own way, I was never alone. Somebody was always pulling me towards France, on the end of that imaginary rope. But we made it, with an amazing amount of support from Eddie the pilot, his team and my good friends Trish, Paul and John who supported me on the pilot boat and for a bit in the water.

I spent less than two minutes on French soil before climbing into a tiny rib and away from the seals. Back on the pilot boat, I brandished my fantastic salt tongue and perfect hat tan line. Jam sandwiches have never tasted so great!

I feel very fortunate to have landed on my feet. After finishing uni, I came to the South Coast to work at the Institute of Naval Medicine with Mike Tipton, who is a professor at the University of Portsmouth and a fount of information about how the human body responds to different environments, including cold water. It was through him that I met the Channel swimmers, so you could say it is all his fault!

Part of what we do is look at ways of improving water-safety messaging for the general public, making people more aware of the problems they may face near water and how they can prevent themselves from getting into difficulty. We also focus on getting across messages around the effects that cold water can have on the body, particularly to people who may not be regular outdoor swimmers; as well as improving athlete welfare in events involving open water, such as triathlons and the Olympic 10k swims. It was through this work that we were given the opportunity to participate in a television programme, *The Doctor Who Gave Up Drugs*, recorded for the BBC. This was in 2015–2016, and involved supporting a young woman to get used to being in cold water, to reduce the cold-shock response (that initial gasp and uncontrolled breathing when you first get in cold water). The woman had lived with depression for a considerable time, and had spent many years on different types of medication. None had really helped her. I think she must have said to somebody that she would try anything to improve her symptoms. And so the wild idea of swimming outdoors in cold water came about. We were there to explain the responses she experienced getting into cold water; to support, monitor and reassure her; and to check she was okay. She spent two days with us, the first day in the lab, discussing the impact of cold water on the body and what would happen to her. Then she had some brief dips in our flume at work. The following day, we took her to a local lake, where she swam with the presenter Dr Chris van Tulleken, Dr Mark Harper and me. From there, we got her swimming with a coach at a lake more local to her. She continued for the rest of that summer and found some reduction in her symptoms, to the point where she was able to come off her medication.

I'd never really seen swimming or being in water as having an impact on my mental health, but it must have done, and does, because it is something that I cling to, and feel refreshed and renewed from. But I could see that others had a strong positive response. Qualitative evidence or narratives of similar stories began to emerge, and are still doing so. Since then, we have been studying not only the potential negative impacts of cold water, but also the potential positives, what effects outdoor swimming may have and for whom. I sincerely hope that this is an area I can work in for the rest of my career.

Water will always be a part of my life. Reflecting, as I have for this piece, I have been gifted some of the most amazing opportunities by so many people and can only thank them for their help and support. I'll continue to seek new adventures, new knowledge and new experiences, and continue to enjoy a short dip or body surfing on waves as much as I do spending hours in the water staring at the fish. But I am also keen to help others experience the water, stay safe in and around water and achieve their goals. I have been privileged to be in the right place at the right time; now it is time for me to support others with their endeavours too.

JO CLEMENT
RHYTHM OF THE OCEAN

Swimming has always been a huge part of my life and I'm guessing it's a love that will continue to grow and deepen until my last breath.

It's hard to talk about my swimming journey without explaining a little bit about my past and my life experiences and influences.

My earliest memories involve time spent in and around the sea with my parents. My father passed his love of the water on to me and he still swims daily in the sea now. He was also a surfer, which meant I had a somewhat transient 'hippy' childhood, moving from town to town across South Africa along the coast in search of the perfect surf, ending up in the famous JBay, before heading to Ireland at the age of fourteen.

After a hard culture shock and move to Ireland, I dropped out of school at fifteen to run away to the UK with an older boyfriend. In my late teens and early twenties, I lost focus in my life and lost my connection to the ocean and to swimming. I struggled to find my way, getting lost on the wrong path … maybe not wrong as I look back now, as it helped carve out the person I have become, and built character and resilience.

Luckily, I found the way back at around the age of twenty-two, going back to college while working full time, then on to study marine and natural history photography and filmmaking at university in Cornwall. However, in my final year of university, I fell pregnant.

The chaos circle seemed to be repeating. After a relationship break-down and becoming a single mother, something had to change. I was not going to let this define my future and I did not want to rely on anyone. I needed to make my own future, and a strong one to support my son.

After working tirelessly when he was a newborn at three different jobs and setting up a photography business, I went self-employed a couple of months after giving birth. Someone told me I was wasting my time and I should get a normal job that was more secure and stop chasing a dream; obviously, I ignored this advice and it made me work even harder to prove them wrong.

It was much later, in my mid-twenties, when I started to return to the rhythm of the water, find balance once again in my own life and have a clearer goal for my future. I had found my focus. I rediscovered my love of the ocean and was making memories with my child.

Long, lonely days away from family, alone with a newborn, were scary, as was setting up a new business with no support. We spent every single day at the beach; come rain or shine, it was our place, where nothing else mattered, where we forgot money worries and all our trou-bles. This was where my love of the ocean and swimming changed again. This time, I had someone to share it with, and I enjoyed seeing his plea-sure of being so free when he was in the sea. Since becoming a mother, I had loved sharing my love of the ocean with my son. My connection to the sea was so strong that I named him Keynvor, which in Cornish means 'ocean', and I love how we can connect with each other and the envi-ronment.

I met my now husband, Patrick, while he was visiting Cornwall from Germany. Our paths collided with full force: he moved to the UK; we joined photography businesses and started another business. Patrick was the missing pieces of my broken puzzle. I introduced him to the sea and swimming and, again, the joy of seeing someone else flourish in this new environment and seeing the amazing effects on them was so beautiful to witness.

I love that our little dysfunctional family can share simple, slow living by swimming. The sea has always drawn me back – it's a place for mind-fulness and my sanctuary in a world that I still find overwhelming and confusing on a daily basis. It's a place to slow down and find focus.

The pressures of modern society, being an adult and now being a parent all come with so much unknown and learning. When I'm feeling it is all too much and the world is moving too fast around me, I find swimming is a great way to reset and help me feel in control of my life again.

It's the same with wild swimming: you don't need a single thing to enjoy the beauty of dipping, splashing, swimming, and so on. That is what I love – you can enjoy it for free. I don't believe in getting caught up in the commercialisation of swimming; trends come and go, fashion comes and goes.

We often swim in our underwear or nude, and dry ourselves with our socks or our T-shirts. I feel most alive being in the elements, and feeling the elements without too much pressure to buy certain things or look a certain way as a 'wild swimmer'. I totally respect other people's decisions, however, in what they choose to buy or wear; this is just my personal viewpoint with everything I do, be that my work life, family life or hobbies.

It's extremely hard to talk about one swim, as we swim so much, but I have a few that have stayed with me.

One of my favourite swims was at sunrise. Patrick and I had been wild camping on a cliff overlooking the sea, on the day before we went into a national lockdown. We woke up to the most magical and dramatic sunrise, the seabirds flying all around us on the edge of the cliff. We scrambled down the rocks to the white sandy beach below as the sun peered over and the low sea mist hovered on the water. We threw off our clothes, running nude into the icy winter seas – ah, it was just the clearest, most beautiful swim I've ever had! It made us completely forget all the world chaos and stress.

Another of my favourite swims was as a family, the three of us at one of our favourite swimming gullies near where we live. We have three freediving masks, which we love for sea swimming. The colours and life you can see beneath you are so mind-blowing and fascinating. I can still see them now: the most beautiful shades of greens, and whites. The seagrass was swaying in the current, moving to some sort of underwater orchestra that we couldn't hear. It was just so beautiful to watch. Then some seals joined us in the bay. I was so happy to have shared this with my family. It was so very basic and simple, but for some reason extremely vivid.

This swim was just at our local harbour of Porthleven, where we swim regularly. My son was having a particularly bad day; I think we all were. There was lots of bickering, moaning and arguing, and I tried to take him on a bike ride to ease his stress and my own. However, we didn't make it very far. We noticed the clear, inviting water of the harbour, so we ended up in our underwear, Keynvor leaping and jumping into the water from the harbour wall, his face a bundle of laughter and delight! We had to dry off with some socks, but we left our worries and bad energy in the sea that day, and came home relaxed and refreshed. The sea is a powerful force.

We always like to say hello to nature, like the sun and the moon (it's pretty weird, I know), to say thank you to the sea and the rivers, to try and remember that we are quite small and insignificant in this big, beautiful planet and that we need to slow down, breathe and actually notice the amazing world in front of us for free.

Social media creates a hugely unrealistic society. Sometimes the slow, simple things for me are the most profound; the free things for us create the most meaningful memories that last a lifetime.

Put the phone away – don't do it for Facebook, don't do it for an Instagram picture; do it for you. Do it to remember, do it to make memories, do it to connect with yourself, do it to connect to the energy that flows all around.

Modern living has taken us further and further away from simple living and knowing how to connect to Mother Earth. We turn on a tap for water, we pop to the local supermarket for food, we turn the heater on for warmth.

That for me is a huge reason why we wild camp and wild swim, away from campsites and pools filled with chemicals, and find more earthy environments away from people. That's where I truly feel most alive – a place I can be free, without distractions or pressure from modern living. Perhaps I was born a century too late.

All of our adventures revolve around where we can swim, and I couldn't imagine a life without the element of water. Long may our water journey continue, along with all the other people who share the same love for swimming, nature's most wonderful free gift.

LES PEEBLES

HELPING OTHERS DISCOVER WILD SWIMMING

In the summer of 2018 I was working, for several weeks, on a decorating job in the Lake District National Park, approximately an hour's commute from my home in the Yorkshire Dales National Park. The sun shone every day as the UK enjoyed a heatwave, and I relished the scenic drive every morning as I crossed from one national park into the one in the next county.

My commute took me past Grasmere lake, and each day it would catch my eye, twinkling in the early morning sunshine, looking so inviting. During that few weeks of work and great weather, the persuasive call of the water became increasingly strong and I promised myself that on the last day of my painting work, a Friday, I would dig out my swim shorts from the far reaches of my wardrobe, dust off the cobwebs and have a dip in Grasmere before I returned home, something I had never done before.

I finished my work and proceeded to take the short drive along the road and park up in a lay-by five minutes from the lake shore. I headed down to the water's edge with my carrier bag in hand, taking in a short woodland walk en route and appreciating the dappled sunlight as I went.

Sitting for a few minutes and sipping from my lukewarm flask of tea, I breathed in the awesome surroundings with woodland behind me, the lake in front of me and high fells framing its far edge. I was just five minutes from the busy road and it seemed I had found myself a little slice of paradise. The water looked so clean and fresh and I imagined it would be very cold – a welcome prospect given I had just finished a hot day's work on the brushes.

Just then, as I was about to get up and get my shorts on, a couple arrived and we exchanged a typically English 'Hiya' and 'What a lovely day' as they began to change into wetsuits. Within a few minutes, they had donned them, packed their dry clothes into a dry bag and got into the water, setting off for a 'proper swim', swimming freestyle and heading northwards towards a small island on the lake which, at a guess, was about a kilometre away.

This was the final encouragement I needed, and when they were just out of sight, I quickly and clumsily got changed, discarding my clothes around my feet, and stood in the water. I was feeling somewhat body-conscious and mildly anxious, but simultaneously I was feeling elated and delighted to be having such an unique experience. The water lapping gently over my ankles was not as cold as I had imagined it would be and so I steadily walked in up to my knees, aiming for a large rock in the water about ten metres from the shoreline. From this vantage point and through the clear water, I could see the lake bed dropping away in front of me and the water appeared to get much deeper and darker, so I decided this would be a good place to launch myself in, slowly. I'd already decided that I wouldn't be swimming any distance, given that it was my first time, and I'd stay close to the rock and tread water and just drink in the experience. Then, just like that, I was in.

In that moment, I was totally awestruck at being fully immersed and surrounded by such a gorgeous landscape, and I allowed myself to turn around 360 degrees, taking it all in. I did this a number of times, as if on a slow merry-go-round. Looking back, I can say it was a sensory delight and I was mostly taken aback by the view from in the water rather than just by it. I felt present and calm in my experience, and my body felt alive and zingy as my workday aches and pains seemingly washed magically away, weightless in every sense. I really couldn't wait to tell my family and, hopefully, get them to return to this gorgeous place with me to try it for themselves. I stayed in the water for maybe five minutes before grabbing my phone and marking my experience with a selfie with the fells as the backdrop – just in case I wasn't believed. When I look back at this photo, I can see I even have some paint on the end of my nose from my earlier work.

I did return the following day with my family, and we enjoyed a picnic and were in and out of the water for several hours – eating and drinking and drying off in between our dips. Needless to say, each of us left the lake that day beaming and feeling happy and well, chatting on the way home about how much we had all enjoyed our time with the lake and each other. I remember us talking about feeling a chill, and saying that our skin felt soft and we felt bright-eyed and bushy-tailed!

As I contemplated our shared experience over the following days, it dawned on me how many happy experiences my family and I had previously had in and by the water, and no matter what our mood when we arrived at the water's edge (be it in a local pool, paddling in a small stream or in the sea on holiday), we always left happy and with an increased sense of well-being and joy. Being by and in water makes many of us happy – fact.

For me personally, the Grasmere experiences had made me happier than I had been for many years, and while I hadn't been particularly low or depressed during that time, my mojo was somewhat depleted. In hindsight, I was firmly stuck in a rather uninspiring cycle of 'work, eat, sleep, repeat' and it felt a little like I lacked purpose and had somehow misplaced or lost the drive I'd had when I was younger. I was okay but not very fulfilled.

These couple of dips ignited something in me quite drastically. I quickly became obsessed with researching, map reading and finding more cold-water locations to have a dip in, and after a short time I realised that I actually lived in a real 'hotspot' for wild swimming in the UK, with a wealth of places to choose from, many on my doorstep. And so my cold-water dipping journey began; within a week or so I was a daily dipper, only missing occasional days due to unsafe river conditions or the busyness of life.

Fast-forward four or so years and I have quite literally completed thousands of dips and swims, alone and in groups large and small. I mostly swim 'skins' (wild swimmers' slang for swim shorts or swimming costume) throughout all seasons. I have swum in heavy rain and blazing sunshine, and have even broken the ice to get into the water to get my cold-water fix. It's been an amazing journey thus far and I have dipped in temperatures ranging from 0.6 °C to 25 °C. Needless to say, I wasn't in for very long at 0.6 °C!

Eighteen months ago, I hung up my painting brushes for the last time and took the leap to become a full-time wild-swimming guide, a job that enables me to share my love of cold water and the beautiful natural world with others both in the Yorkshire Dales and the Lake District, and it's been a fabulous decision which has been both life-changing and life-enhancing for me and my family. I wake most mornings feeling very lucky to have such an amazing job where I get to share the joy of something I love with others. Some days, I take groups of visiting wild swimmers from all over the UK to some of my favourite swim spots, and sometimes I give people a first-time experience of the cold water, showing them how they can get started safely. It really is a huge privilege to share these things with others and to have a shared experience that brings much happiness to them and to me. I regularly hear new folk say that they feel better than they have done for a long while and, of course, I can totally relate to this, given where my own journey began.

Introducing folk to the cold water is a summer highlight for me as I get to witness and enjoy their initial steps. I meet them by the river and I can often detect a slight terror in their faces, and they will typically voice their anxieties and worries within a few moments. 'Will it be cold?' they might ask. I see it as my responsibility to help them slow down and enjoy the whole experience, and before we get to the spot we are to swim in, I will often take a very short detour to show them an amazing waterfall because it's a distraction from their fast-paced thoughts and their worries. The pace of life we have these days is, in my opinion, unsustainable long term, and so a priority for me is to help each person learn to slow right down. Wild swimming or dipping doesn't have to be a race or about far we can go – for me, the cold-water dipping is an opportunity to slow down and even extract myself from that busyness.

The waterfall is an opportunity for them to stop and see nature in action and I tell them how, once a year, the salmon jump up this triple waterfall after swimming about 2,000 miles on an empty stomach through salt and fresh water before spawning further upstream. I also take the opportunity to speak a little of how the river is moving in all directions, and how, after heavy rain, levels can rise dramatically and move huge trees and boulders above and below the water. I want them to love it, and I also want them to know what a powerful element the water can be and leave my session with a healthy respect for the wild waters – which, as we all know, can be extremely dangerous. We then take the short three-minute walk to the riverbank, where we change and begin our intro session. The nerves are still there and so I gently remind them to take their time, to enjoy the experience and to metaphorically 'smell the flowers'. I encourage them to place their towels and dry clothes where they can find them easily and to feel free to look around and take photos of the gorgeous surroundings we are in. What I know is that this stretch of river is a bucket-list swim for many, and experienced dippers will travel hundreds of miles for a ten-minute dip here – it is simply magical and ever-changing. I'm lucky enough to call this my local stretch of river.

When the group are all clad in their swimwear, we ease into the water, up to our ankles, our knees and our belly buttons before fully immersing ourselves with our chins on the water's mirror-like surface, all the while taking great care to check that our breathing is neither gasping or shallow, but just normal. The screeches and screams and ooohs and aaahs can be hilarious and I've learnt many a swear word from these sessions, all delivered in good spirit and great fun. As they get fully in with their feet planted on the river bed, I joke that they are not thinking about their ankles any more. It's now I tell them how deep this stretch of river is and that, when we are ready, we will swim across its width, about fifteen metres, but we will stop in the middle and tread water and have a good look at where we are; and then, just like that, their wild-swimming journey begins, slowly and wonderfully. Within moments of swimming together, I see their countenance change, going from slight terror to relaxing, feeling held and being delighted that they are doing it. This is always a special moment for me.

'You never regret a dip' is also something I've heard a lot during the last few years in the swimming community, and it's true – I don't regret even one of my dips. That said, some dips are more satisfying or prettier than others, but the cold water is always an excellent conductor of peace, happiness and joy, which continues to help me feel alive and well. I know this is the same for others too, including people with chronic illnesses searching for, and finding, temporary relief from their symptoms; and those experiencing grief receiving moments of peace and quietness from their immersion in cold water.

As I have reflected on my own journey with cold-water dipping and swimming, I can honestly tell you that my mental and physical well-being feels like it has increased significantly – this is my personal experience and feeling, and not based on any study, record-keeping or science. I know I feel happier and healthier, I have more peace and I'm braver and more courageous than I can ever remember. I've also wondered why this is so, and while I am no expert, it's my belief that immersing myself in cold water gently shocks me, mentally and physically, into being fully present in the moment – in other words, the water is so cold that I simply can't think of the 101 other things I may have to do that day or about my anxieties, and this is a type of wonderful respite – which in turn is relieving and even healing. Cold water is certainly not a magic wand to wash away all of one's issues or problems, but – for me anyway – it gives me what I need: a boost of energy and perspective, allowing me to continue on my own path as best as I can. I hear this is the same for others too.

Another very important part of my wild-swimming and mental-health journey is that of community. Today the wild-swimming community is huge throughout the world, and what a lovely community I have experienced it to be. I believe that a shared experience of dipping in cold water is like no other and it's a real leveller. Our usual masks of composure that we all tend to hold up day to day are temporarily washed away by the water, allowing each of us just to be who we are in that moment. I happen to think this is a primary and healthy foundation for genuine community to build, and to this end I have had many peak experiences with others in the water, sometimes in silence, sometimes accompanied by heartfelt conversation or laughter.

KATE STEELS

THE ICE SEVENS

Open-water swimming, and in particular ice swimming, has become a key part of my life. Through swimming, I have developed in so many ways. I have made some amazing friends, pushed personal physical boundaries, introduced others to and coached them in this amazing sport, and travelled to some exotic locations. Very importantly, it has really helped me cope with the devastating loss of my only child, Daniel, who was just nineteen years old when he tragically died.

In November 2021, I became the first person in the UK and third in the world to complete the ultimate ice-swimming challenge – the Ice Sevens. This comprises swimming a mile in water of 5 °C or less wearing only a costume, cap and goggles in each continent, including a polar region and an 'Ice Zero' below 1 °C.

I feel very privileged and proud to have achieved this and to have been named the World Open Water Swimming Association's Woman of the Year 2021.

My first ice mile was at Andark Lake in Hampshire in 2015, two months before the inaugural Ice Swimming World Championships in Murmansk, Russia. I had been training hard to acclimatise and attempt the ice mile. Andark Diving Centre had recently completed their small man-made lake designed for diver training, combined with superb and warm lakeside facilities. I recollect walking around the lake with the owners, asking for permission to train there. At this time, ice swimming and cold-water swimming wasn't 'a thing'. I was given permission in return for raising money for a marine conservation charity. I organised the ice mile itself, including safety, medical requirements and all the paperwork. I found the swim tough, but was euphoric afterwards. A seed had been planted in my head. This was the sport for me! I have continued to work with Andark to help develop the lake as an all-year-round swimming venue. In 2016 they hosted the first IISA (International Ice Swimming Association) GB championships.

The ice-swimming community and friendships within it are close knit. Sometimes the very best plans are formed at events. It was after an IISA event that Ger Kennedy invited me to his polar ice-swimming expedition to the very north of Norway – just over seventy degrees north. Our base was at the stunning Mikkelvik Brygge in a brand new complex of lodges. The views from our lodge were breathtaking, with mountains covered in thick snow surrounded by crystal-clear icy seas. Special memories were formed – friendship, teamwork and laughter; the most spectacular scenery combined with dancing Northern Lights displays. I also remember the sea urchins – I had never really considered they would survive in cold arctic waters, but they were everywhere.

For my African ice mile, I went to the high Atlas Mountains with my partner, Rory, and another very good friend, Matthew Johnston. The plan was for all of us to swim an ice mile, but once we got there the men backed out. Again, I had to plan all the logistics, including finding a Moroccan guide and a medic from the Red Cross. I was grateful for the advice and tips from my good friend and Ice Queen Jaimie Monahan.

On the planned day of the attempt, we arrived late morning. It was a sunny day with a little snow on the opposite side of the lake. My guide had arranged for the caretaker of a very dilapidated old mansion to open the doors and light a wonderful fire for me to rewarm. Unfortunately, the sun had pushed the shallow waters just over 5 °C, so it became a training swim. We spent the rest of the day exploring other potential options. We had alternative possibilities, but Lake Aguelmame Sidi Ali remained my favourite. That night, a severe frost was forecast. Excellent! Up in the mountains, it was even colder. A super early start and heavy frost meant I had the magic temperature and was able to complete my ice mile.

Later that same month, December 2017, I was given an opportunity to represent IISA as an official in Shuangyashan, China. I jumped at the opportunity. It was early in the season coming from the UK and the water was 0 °C. I had already swum several one-kilometre events in 0 °C, but had my eye on an ice zero after the event.

The journey to Shuangyashan was complicated. The agreement was that we would fly to the Harbin in the far north of China (an amazing city with an annual ice festival) to meet Russian friends. There were no direct flights to Harbin and we landed in -30 °C without our luggage. From experience I had two cossies, goggles and hats in my hand luggage, but not much else. Our Russian friends took us to Decathlon to buy thermals and clothing, although the choice was very limited as almost everything was small or extra small! The next problem was that Decathlon only accepted cash and we didn't have enough, but our Russian friends saved the day. We dashed via a cashpoint to the train station for a very long and not particularly comfortable sixteen-hour train journey, not the best way to get over jetlag and prepare for a swimming competition.

The Chinese made us feel incredibly welcome and we were given some amazing art gifts. The swimming venue was a twenty-five-metre pool cut out of a frozen lake, fairly remote and exposed to the wind. There was an incredible structure built for the first event: high diving. The Chinese seem to love diving. They started all the events as if we were in a heated pool with dive starts and tumble turns!

After the event, and after a lot of quite lively discussion with the Chinese referee, medics and our Russian friends, two of us were allowed to attempt an ice mile. This was the hardest swim of my life. It pushed me to my limit. Not only was the water 0 °C but the wind chill was -22 °C. I had no dryrobe and so borrowed one which was far too small. The Crocs didn't fit, so walking up steps at the end was almost impossible. An Ice Zero is so different to a 'standard' ice mile – so much tougher and longer. The harder the swim, the harder the recovery. I had total faith in my recovery team, in particular Alexander Brylin and Rory. I am a huge fan of the Russian method of rewarming: in summary, put your hands and feet in a bucket of cold water while having hot towels wrapped around your kidneys, groin and armpits before eventually going into a sauna.

I was quickly whisked out of the sauna – it was time to move on. As I exited the changing rooms, I had a TV interview in the freezing air before being ushered into our minibus. The only vacant seat was at the back.

The heater didn't work and the inside of the windows were frozen. Within an hour, I requested a toilet stop, but it was denied. The Chinese organisers were in a rush – we thought to get to our hotel. Eventually we stopped – not for me but because we needed fuel and the Russians wanted vodka. Relief! We were quickly on our way again, and instead of a hotel, we were issued train tickets and put on an overnight train to our next destination, where we put on an ice-swimming display.

For my North American ice mile, I headed to Beaverton, a small town on the shores of Lake Simcoe, Canada. My swim had been postponed by six months following the death of my beloved son. I knew I had to keep swimming and get in the ice to help me cope. I had planned most of the swim. St John Ambulance provided my medical cover and local ice swimmers helped provide safety cover and support. The most memorable thing from this swim was the community support from the whole of Beaverton, who came out to watch me swim. A neighbour's daughter was a photographer and made a professional short video which I will always treasure. Another neighbour let me use their sauna to finish rewarming. The other thing I remember about Lake Simcoe was the shifting ice. We stayed at the lakeside in a wonderful Airbnb. The lake is massive and the melt was well underway. There were large sheets of ice breaking and being pushed by the wind. On the first day, there was about fifty metres of breaking ice packed up against the shore, squeaking and cracking loudly. With the help of local ice swimmer Josef, we went looking for alternative locations, as I could not get to clear water from Beaverton. We planned to swim at Josef's town of Barrie. The beach is lovely but was too far for the community to come and watch. I felt guilty explaining this to our hosts, but there was nothing else we could do.

I slept well. We got up and went to the lakeside. It was unbelievable: the ice had gone! Then, almost simultaneously, I got a call from Josef saying Barrie beach was impossible as it was full of ice. In the end, I had perfect conditions: flat, calm, sunny and great temperature. Towards the end, I had to negotiate a mini iceberg that floated into the course, but my kayaker guided me around it.

It was at this time that I started to believe that I could achieve the Ice Sevens but needed a sponsor. I work full-time in local government, but my pay is poor. Training takes up a lot of time, as does IISA GB work and organising national championships.

In August 2019, I managed to scrape together enough money to go to New Zealand. Rory had a good friend, Simon Olliver, with whom he used to swim in the UK before he emigrated, and put me in touch. Simon and Ely were fantastic, and I owe them so much for my Oceanic ice mile. They let me stay, took me for a recce into the alps beforehand and had all the connections for safety and medics. Lake Lyndon is in an idyllic location. I had opted for an A-to-B swim, the only ice mile I have done that way (with exit points all the way along). It seemed forever in the water, especially as the wind picked up during the swim.

I had found it really hard to acclimatise. July and August in the UK were blisteringly hot. I struggled to keep my ice bath below 5 °C in the garden. I don't like ice baths, but needs must. The seas in Christchurch were 7–8 °C and I had a week's intensive acclimatisation, swimming one mile two or three times a day. I also retained some acclimatisation from the previous season.

I didn't manage to complete my South American ice mile until two years later. I had difficulty finding a sponsor, but then AXA Insurance supported me. I am hugely thankful to them. I was considering various locations. Then, in 2020, the Covid pandemic and lockdowns hit. South America kept its borders shut much longer than Europe. I had to be patient.

Unexpectedly, I got diagnosed with a brain aneurysm. I had to undergo major surgery in January 2021 – at the height of wave two of Covid in the UK and before vaccines were readily available. To say I was scared is an understatement. The operation itself is high-risk, but if I had caught Covid I knew I wouldn't come out. My surgeons were amazing and after a very tough recovery, I was told I could swim again. It took a long time to regain fitness, but I had a goal: my South American ice mile.

Chile and Argentina remained locked down. After about six weeks of negotiating with the Falkland Islands government and immigration department, with formal support from my MP, IISA and my doctor, I was finally granted an exceptional permit to enter and travel on a military flight to attempt my final ice mile. My ice bath became my best friend again. However, within six days of my flight, there had been a formal objection and my permit was revoked. I was gutted. The roller-coaster journey continued.

I was still watching entry restrictions in Argentina and Chile, but had resigned myself to having to wait until spring 2022. Argentina opened its borders on 1 November. Unexpectedly, I was contacted by Luis Argemonte, to whom I had been chatting for a long time through Facebook. He said there were two glacial lakes with sufficiently cold water – but I needed to get there asap and before December. I sorted out logistics with work. Booking flights was tricky as there were no direct options (Antarctica was reopening, so flights were full and very expensive). Ushuaia was amazing and Luis welcomed us so warmly into his family. I trained hard for a week in the Beagle Channel. The weather was warming up, but the forecast was for gale-force winds on Saturday, my swim day. I rescheduled for Sunday. Nerves really set in …

On Saturday night, eight to ten centimetres of snow fell. Luis asked me if I still wanted to attempt it or whether we should postpone to Tuesday. I felt ready and decided to go ahead. I had my support crew and doctor. Psychologically, I thought Tuesday could be a reserve date in case I didn't make it. We set off into the mountains just outside the national park (you can't swim in the national park). It was early and we were at Lake Esmeralda long before the tourists and trekkers arrived. It was snowing softly, with only a thin covering of fresh snow. It was magical! While others measured and marked the swim course, I put the tent up and became increasingly nervous.

I started the swim. I thought of Dan, the rest of my family, Rory, everyone who had helped me on my journey, and my support team on the shore. I tried to settle into the swim. It took until well over one kilometre before I seemed to get into a rhythm. I always slow around the 1,200–1,400-metre mark, but tried to focus on my stroke. At 1,400 metres, I could almost sense the finish, but I wouldn't let myself believe it – I was telling myself just to focus on my stroke or otherwise I might get cramp, or swallow water. Then I was at the finish line and heard a massive cheer. I felt really strong and could have easily kept going! My recovery was good. I soon became my normal chatty self and my support team said I was a different person on the hike back – clearly totally relaxed and extremely happy!

MIKAYLA GUIDERA

FREEZBRURY

The thought of swimming in cold open water in Ireland made me laugh. I used to think, 'Are you mad?' 'Not a chance!' This is exactly how I felt when I was asked to take part in the Freezbrury challenge in January 2020. For those who don't know, the Freezbrury is a cold-water immersion challenge, started by Damian Browne, which raises money for mental health charities in Ireland. The idea of this challenge is to immerse yourself in cold water every day in February, starting off with one minute on the 1st, two minutes on the 2nd, and so on every day up to twenty-eight minutes on the 28th, or in my case twenty-nine minutes as it was a leap year. There are no wetsuits allowed and no hats or gloves, just a swimsuit. You must also fully submerge yourself under the water at least once.

Naturally, when I was asked to do this challenge I laughed at the idea and said absolutely no way was I going to do it. There was no chance that I would be able to handle that. With a lot of persuasion from my personal trainer and friend Neil, I reluctantly said yes, on the condition I would just try it the first day. I never planned on making it to day two – I would never be able to do it. I loved swimming but in a heated pool or a warm sea, not in a river. I had heard there was a group of people doing it, but I did not know who they were or what kind of people they would be. I was more nervous about the people than the challenge.

I grew up on an estate beside the river and I spent my summer days swimming in the river, no matter what the weather was like, but this was in summer, not February. I absolutely love the water, but it had been a long time since I was in it and you are a lot more fearless as a kid than as an adult.

As the day approached, I was getting more and more nervous, not only about whether the water was going to be freezing but about what I was going to wear. As a plus-size woman, the thought of putting on a swimsuit was extremely intimidating. I was freaking out the night before, trying to find something to wear. I was so worried about what people would think if I just wore a swimsuit: was I too fat to be around people I didn't even know in just a swimsuit, would they pass comment, would they laugh, would they judge? I look back and laugh that that was my biggest worry and not the fact I was getting into cold water in Ireland in February. I ended up wearing a swimsuit, but I wore shorts and a vest top over it and I felt slightly better about myself.

As I looked at the cold water of the River Nore on 1 February 2020, I had absolutely no idea how I was about to change my life. It was a nice day weather-wise, a little bit chilly but dry, and for Ireland that is all you can really ask for. As I was trying to psych myself up, I just grew more and more nervous. I made the mistake of putting my hand in to check how cold it was – that's just silly, don't do that! I finally got changed into my swimwear and prepared to take the plunge. After a lot of screaming and trying to run, I stopped and had a word with myself. I reminded myself of the reason I was doing the challenge. I was going to raise much-needed money for mental health charities, which are very close to my heart. It was going to be a challenge of mind over matter.

I cannot describe that feeling of getting in for the first time. Yes, it was freezing, and even though it was only for one minute, I didn't think I would last. Again, I reminded myself why I was doing it. People who struggle with their mental health are always fighting a constant battle. You need to keep fighting; however, the fight can be made easier when you surround yourself with the right people, and that was exactly what I was going to do. I turned to my friend and just laughed. 'What are we doing?' There were people on the other side of the river cheering us on, and before I knew it the timer went off and I jumped out of the river. My body was red and I was shivering, but I was so happy. I couldn't wait to do it again. Once my body defrosted and I was sitting on the bank of the river wrapped up in a blanket and having a cup of coffee, I felt different. I felt incredible.

I had a sense of calm about me for the rest of the day. My mind was at ease. I felt I was more productive in my day after the swim. I had a clear head and felt like I had hit a reset button on my mind, body and soul. I was so excited for the next day. If I was able to do one minute, then two minutes would be even better. I felt different going into day two – all my worries were gone. Who cared what I looked like, I was just excited to feel that post-dip feeling again. I rocked a swimsuit the next day and didn't even bat an eyelid at what people thought. It takes a certain group of people to do this challenge, each as mad as the next, but being judgemental was not on the cards. It didn't take long for me to end up wearing a bikini and I have never looked back. It is a benefit of swimming I don't hear people talking about too much, but my confidence has gone through the roof. The swimming community, both in person and online, has been so incredible on this journey. I am not an advocate for 'every body is a bikini body'. I encourage people to embrace their bodies and just enjoy the swim.

As the challenge went on, it wasn't easy. The dark nights and the many storms we faced were a true test, but we all got through it, together. The most amazing part was that when you are sitting in a river for twenty-plus minutes with people you have just met, you start to talk, you get to know people's stories, you share yours. We had all kinds of weather that February, and it just added to the challenge. The days I might have been struggling, there was always somebody there to help me push through it (except the day with the frog, but that's a whole different story!), or I was there to help somebody else. It was a lesson in dealing with my own mental health, which I didn't realise at the time. Don't get me wrong, every day I got to the river, I still struggled to get in. I knew that after it I was going to feel amazing, but let's be real here, it was so cold! Some days we had water temperatures of 2 °C and air temperatures of -3 °C. Nowadays, I sometimes run into the water like it's Hawaii and other days it takes me a long time to get in. It is all in my head – like a lot of things in life, the thought of it is a lot worse than it ends up being.

During my time doing this challenge, I started to realise that it would be very helpful to have the right gear. That is one piece of advice I would give to anybody who is considering starting. Preparation is key. I found a new little Irish clothing brand in August 2020: HUH Clothing donates money to mental health charities. I had to buy some hoodies to keep me warm after my swim, so why not support a local business and help contribute to charity too?

Fast-forward to now and swimming is just a part of who I am. I like to call myself 'the plus-size mermaid'. I have met some of the most amazing people since I began, some in person and some online. The swimming community is literally the greatest in the world. There is nothing quite like getting out of the water, getting warm again and sitting around having a chat over a hot drink. I find most people who enjoy year-round cold-water swimming are usually similar. I know almost everybody in their lifetime will more than likely deal with mental health issues, and there is no one way to deal with them. For a lot of us, it is the water, it's the shock of the cold, it's the sense of calm, it's the people you meet, it's the reason to get out of bed and go do something, it's being out in nature. Whatever it may be, don't knock it until you've tried it. I have never regretted a swim.

KATHLEEN WOTTON

THE SEA SAVED ME

During lockdown in 2020, while scrolling through social media, I found cold-water swimming by chance, as well as rediscovering my love of country music that was instilled in me as a child. I'd given up on living; everything was way beyond my control. I began a waiting game, enduring sheer emotional and physical despair, just waiting to fade off to sleep eternally. But my lost hope became a tower of strength and tenacity to fight for life.

A little about me, just me. My name is Kathleen, Katie for short. I am forty-nine years old. A mum, nana, sister, daughter and auntie. I've spent my life doing good by others. I've a keen interest in health and studied hard over the years. In lockdown 2020, I was way over forty-five stone. I'd always lived under the shadow of poor self-worth, which started very early in my childhood. As a child, I'd always felt a sense of social awkwardness that was picked up by and heightened by bullies. I remember listening to country music with my nana and getting lost in the lyrics, giving me so much comfort. My biggest regret was letting my physical and mental health drag me to the lowest point in my life. Depression took its hold, but it took greater strength to recognise my flaws and let them drift away in the ocean tide. The roots that bound my low mood inside were thicker than ever before, turning and churning within dark thoughts, forever tugging and pulling so hard that I'd forgotten how to fight for me and had given up completely.

The moment I truly became connected with the real me was during lockdown. I finally found a fight for the lost child inside me. Scrolling through Facebook as I lay on the sofa, I was unable to bear my own weight for longer than three seconds, constantly crying with pain.

With one click, I accidentally stumbled on a country singer, Paul Holley, who has become a friend for life, inspiring me to keep moving on. There was something in Paul's voice that stunned me deep inside. I felt a shockwave of life burst through every inch of my being with so much energy, sinking my body beneath the ocean's breath. The water gave me a huge relief from the sheer anguish and pain that I'd lived with for longer than I care to remember, free from all the burdens that had led me to forsake my very own well-being.

The turning point came like a wave crashing against the shore. Suddenly, out of the blue, a positive pull connected me to the ocean with a tug so hard that I had to go with the waves. It felt like the negative roots had been snapped and I began to wake up and pay attention. Scrolling further, I saw a photo of two of my siblings, Sarah and Christine, swimming in the sea alongside friends. I cried so much, as it brought back so many happy memories as a child at my favourite place; my life felt real when I was swimming in the sea.

I did it. I swam in the sea again. When the dark clouds became so thick and black that I thought I would never rise again, just seeing that one photo resonated through vessels to my heart and became the music to guide me into the sea once more, reliving every morsel of happiness I had experienced as a child. The sound of the ocean waves, with the smell of the salt and seaweed I once loved, was ringing sheer delight through me. Taking that leap to swap the blackness for the ice-cold blue and green sea saved me. Every hurdle I have climbed has been a stepping stone to discover the magic of the ocean depths. Time stood still as the tide sloshed over my toes and a beautiful cold breeze rang through my ears. My skin was on fire, tingling and smarting with the immense sensation of the ocean as it comforted me from the pain like a warm fleece blanket on a cold winter's day. Time stood still.

I remember most vividly the moment that I tried to walk across the sand as my feet slipped with an unsteady balance, my legs wobbling and the pain intensifying with every move I made. The distance was just yards, but all I could envisage was sheer miles, and the agonising task seemed way beyond my comprehension and capabilities. My body leant so far forward that I'd shrunk inches, my back bent and twisted. In such a short time, the sea has given so much more than I ever could have thought. I am now climbing like a sunflower in the midst of summer, learning to bloom and shine like the morning sun. I am no longer a wilting weed but as beautiful as a flower in full bloom, sparkling brighter and brighter with every day that passes.

When the dark days come, I shall never succumb to the sadness that held on to me. I am learning how to be happy just as me, beautiful just as I am. I no longer need another to confirm this, as the ocean kept my heart beating and my love shines from deep inside. I now believe that no one could set a burden upon my shoulders. I love easily from my heart and soul; I don't judge before I see the whole book in any living soul. People are beautiful from the inside out and not from what's on the surface only. I am larger than life in more ways than one. The ocean embraces every-one, no matter what their appearance.

The sea is free and full of magic. It offers hope and dignity to all, in so many ways. Now over twenty stone lighter, I'm free and brighter and want nothing more than to support and help others to find their anchor in order to help themselves or stay motivated, to grab life and keep living for today and onwards. My advice to all is to take that leap of faith, no matter how small or big. Trying is better than giving up and not living. I have hurdles that I have not overcome; they are not my failures but my desires to keep swimming and smiling and fighting for life.

I love just being me and will never let hardships overwhelm me; my true child will always shine inside out. So, with a swoop and a dive beneath the sea, I emerge as so much more than I ever thought I could possibly be. Stay safe and embrace what Mother Nature brings to you.

LORETTA COX

DISCOVERING OPEN-WATER
SWIMMING

To explain my take on mental health and open-water swimming, you need to understand why I started open-water swimming in the first instance.

Back in 1995, I had gone through a messy divorce and was figuring out how I could exist with my two children and what that would look like. Going through the divorce, I lost the marital home and had to sell it. My husband generously gave me the home to bring up our children, but shortly after signing over the house to me, the rail network drew up plans for the Channel Tunnel line to be built. It was going to come above ground just in front of the house about 300 metres away – near enough that it devalued the house to a point where I had to sell without any equity. That was problem number one.

I had also just lost my father, and with the stress of everything it was a wonder I was functioning at all. I saw the problems looming and contacted the council to say I would shortly be homeless along with my two small children; thankfully, a little while later they found me a housing association property in Westerham, Kent.

I was worried all the time, both financially and physically. I was at Royal Mail, which had been a godsend. My hours of work, combined with having an au pair – although financially draining – allowed me to have more time with my children.

I desperately needed some time for myself, for my sanity as much as anything else. A few years before, I had had an accident on my delivery bike which affected my ability to run. In fact, doctors said I was not to run ever again. This was beginning to make me feel depressed, as running was a huge part of my life which had been curtailed.

Looking for another alternative that I could immerse myself in fully, I returned to the doctors' surgery to ask if it really was their final decision on running and what might be a feasible alternative. The answers were not positive, but would on reflection give true meaning to living.

As I walked home thinking over what the doctor had said, a plan started to evolve. The doctor said I would be able to swim. However, at thirty-nine years of age, I could not envisage competing in a pool. My mind wandered to Channel swimming, a real challenge and a real possibility. On arriving home, I immediately jumped into action and contacted the Channel Swimming Association. It wasn't long before I had spoken to the relevant people, got a training plan and found a charity to swim for who also had a pool I could use. Everything fell into place.

However, not long after, while immersed in training, I felt unwell. With some tests it was discovered I had cancer in the tissue behind my womb. More worry – plus, shortly after my surgery to remove said cancer, my mother passed away. After undergoing triple bypass surgery, she was not recovering but existing on machines. As a family, we decided to turn off the machines, as we knew that wasn't how my mother would want to exist.

It was a devastating blow on top of everything that had happened over the previous months. I wasn't coping too well. My go-to place was swimming.

A few months later, around Easter time, I had resumed my arduous training, but in the sea at Dover with all the other Channel-swimming aspirants.

At first, never really having swum at sea, I was to be honest wondering why anybody in their right mind would ever contemplate swimming in cold water, in salt and with constant changes of conditions. I soon found out why … oh my word, swimming in the sea puts a whole new meaning into feeling alive!

There were of course the obvious differences: no lane markers, ends, chlorine, confinement rules or regulations. But there was so much more:

waves to play in, currents to pit yourself against, the warmth of the sun on your skin – I love that bit! The changing scenery was one thing I had never realised would be a factor, but it is, plus swimming in differing conditions never ceased to thrill.

I found myself utterly smitten with the whole concept of open-water swimming. I have had so many adventures beyond swimming the English Channel, which I could never have perceived when I first dreamt of swimming as a way of stopping me falling head first into a deep depression.

Now I have become an open-water coach, have trained many aspiring Channel swimmers, and have moved to Cornwall – which in itself is inspiring because of the hundreds of beautiful swim locations – but the dream goes on. That's the beauty of open-water swimming: it's as big as your imagination. I now know what it is I like about open water. I look for swim events, either organised or imagined, and apply myself fully. Sometimes, though, just swimming for myself for my own enjoyment is the order of the day and I don't train at all. On these occasions, I find a lovely Cornish beach with good visibility and calm waters. Then I'm very content to swim slowly, watching the rippling sand go by within my line of vision. I love to see kelp and seaweed, something I previously had to overcome my fear of. I love seeing crabs scuttling across the bottom or a small school of fish float by – all very calming. Being at one with the ocean is a real privilege which I feel deeply. I respect its power but love with every fibre its allure.

SARAH KENNEDY NORQUOY

SWIMMING TO RESET

It was 1 May 2019 and my alarm went off at 4.20 a.m., something unheard of in my world. But on this occasion I jumped to life and was up and out of my bed before I had time to invite my brain into the discussion about whether I wanted to do this or not. My brain wasn't allowed an opinion at this point – there's too much sanity involved if my brain kicks in – I was completely driven by my heart and my soul was doing all the talking. So, yes, I definitely wanted to do this, however crazy the 'this' might seem.

Beltane is a Gaelic festival held between the spring equinox and summer solstice, usually on 1 May. It signifies the return of summer, and in ancient days, festivals took place to say goodbye to the darkness and welcome the new light, some warmth and animals going out to pasture. In Orkney it was traditional to wash your face in the morning dew to aid health, happiness and youthful looks. I was going to need a robust amount of dew to achieve this for me, so instead I went for immersing myself in the sea at sunrise, a tradition followed by much of the outdoor-swimming community I later came to discover. I'd not been swimming outdoors for long at this point. Having only started a few months earlier, I'd quickly become hooked and felt the benefits in a multitude of ways, both physically and mentally. Having lost a close friend to cancer and seen my mother diagnosed with dementia within the space of two weeks, I needed something to help me cope with all the grief that life was throwing at me, and swimming outdoors in very cold temperatures quickly became the thing to restore and reset me on an almost daily basis.

While the world slept, I made the twenty-minute drive to the chosen beach in Evie, Orkney, to meet the other swimmers. The atmosphere was magical as the light began to show itself, the tranquillity of the sea breathtaking. It was misty, calm and totally serene. Everyone spoke in hushed tones, not wanting to break the magic. The salty air was crisp and cold and the horizon shrouded in mist. We entered the water, letting out squeals as the water lapped around us, pushing our body temperatures down and causing us to breathe slowly and calmly while our bodies adjusted.

Curious seals stuck their heads up to see what was happening. We trod water silently while they investigated us before disappearing into the ocean and swimming off. The sun was a little shy that morning, hiding behind the clouds and only offering the merest of orange tinges, but we didn't care. It was just fabulous to be in the vast blue space and away from the daily grind, even if only for twenty minutes.

We dressed hurriedly, shivering and pouring hot drinks before getting into our cars and heading off in various directions to rejoin the waking world and go about our day.

I have swum many, many times since that swim – hundreds if not thousands – but this one is particularly memorable and goes down as one of my favourites. I can still recall driving home and smiling to myself as I shook my head, saying out loud, 'You've lost your mind!' I remember being giddy with excitement at what I had just done; my heart was full. I had never felt so alive.

'I wish I had found this sooner.'
'Yes, but it wasn't your time.'

I often return to this brief exchange, which took place in the water in January 2019 when I first began my sea-swimming journey. Swimming quickly became a lifeline for me.

Wild swimming, sea swimming, cold-water swimming, outdoor swimming, whatever you want to call it, is hugely popular now since the pandemic shut all the indoor pools and people took to the outdoors and quickly discovered what all the fuss was about. I started before the wild-swimming revolution took off, as a response to a low-key midlife crisis. My children had both left home, I was in the last year of my forties and I had spent the previous year attending various medical and hospital appointments with my mother, resulting in a dementia diagnosis. CT scans, psychiatry appointments and memory tests simply confirmed what I already knew, but to hear it officially was devastating, as was watching someone who was once a force to be reckoned with deteriorate irreversibly.

My life was sandwiched between ageing parents and children who had recently left home, who still needed me but in a different way. I felt pulled in a million directions and spread thinner than a cigarette paper. I was overwhelmed with the enormity of everything, and entering the water brought me mental respite, calm and moments of joy. I started to feel better about myself in a multitude of ways. I've long been in a complicated relationship with my body, but now I began to feel a sense of pride in what it could achieve. I felt empowered by my ability to keep doing this thing: put mind over matter and get into cold water, sometimes as snow lay on the ground or ice floated on the surface. I became addicted to the post-swim buzz as every nerve in my body fought to warm me back up again. I enjoyed connection with others, scenery, wildlife and the sounds of gulls above me. And I felt reset, every single time.

When it comes to mental health, wild swimming has worked wonders for me, which has enabled me to keep doing it for over three years now, never having missed a week, sometimes going in up to three times a day.

I've swum in all weathers, in many locations, and at all different times of the day and night. On many occasions, I've found myself standing at the water's edge wondering what the heck I'm doing before wading in and having the cold take my breath away, but not once have I regretted it when I exit, exhilarated and renewed.

I'm not saying wild swimming is the cure-all. But it's certainly the cure for many things. As a late bloomer, starting aged forty-nine, I can't imagine a life without it now.

I've read many accounts by people who have found renewed life from immersing themselves in nature and finding water to swim in. I would even go so far as to say it's been life-changing for me. I went on to write a book about it, as the experience was so incredible I wanted to add voice to it. If you're wanting to give it a try but feel nervous, I can completely identify with this. I was incredibly nervous before my first swim, but with encouragement from friends and a bit of screeching and squealing initially, I quickly found a coping mechanism for life that cannot be matched. Try it for yourself.

RACHEL ASHE
TRYING TO FIT

A few years ago, my mind was in chaos. I lived in fear, terrified that people would see behind my smiley mask as I swung between huge emotions which made me feel disoriented most of the time.

As a child, some really awful things happened to me and my mind turned to dissociation as a way to cope. Some memories fell down a black hole and others got muddled and worried me. When I felt a big emotion, I'd switch off, forget, feel confused and then be deeply ashamed. It's only as I've gotten older that I can look back and see how unwell I really was.

Being a human felt like an impossible task. I was a round peg that desperately wanted to fit into a square hole. However, being an adopted, mixed-race person in a white family meant I was never going to.

Now, I'm sure you're thinking that this will be a story of how cold water saved my life and made all my problems wash away. In some ways, you're kind of right.

The truth is, it took ten years of therapy and lots and lots of hard work and a mixture of medication, making positive changes in my life – but, yes, cold water is where the magic really happened.

In 2018 I was staying with my parents in Edinburgh for Christmas. It had been a few months since receiving my diagnosis from my psychiatrist and I was trying out medication which had horrible side effects. I'd got through it by taking sedatives during the day and sleeping pills at night. I felt numb and deeply sad. I was worried about the future, about being a good mum, about feeling isolated because whenever I felt unwell, I avoided my friends.

In Edinburgh there's a big New Year's Day dip every year called the 'Loony Dook'. I don't know why I did it but I decided that I would go and join in. There were hundreds of people there. Lots of people with hangovers standing round the bonfire in different states of undress, getting into wetsuits or jogging on the spot hugging themselves or blowing into their hands. I stood to the side in my black M&S tummy-control swimsuit, pulling it down over my bum and tucking my boobs into the top.

When the crowd gathered in a long line across the beach, I joined them. I half walked, half jogged down to the sea with one arm across my chest to stop myself from wobbling straight out of my swimsuit. I went into the water and it was so cold it hurt.

I was only in there a minute and then back out, dripping up the sand. The pain was horrible. Yet, as I started to thaw, I felt something wash over me. I felt like the numbness was gone; I felt a glimmer of hope again. I went into the cold water and it somehow sparked a fire in me.

Cold water gave me a purpose. Like most of the cold-water lovers these days, I wanted to go around and tell everybody how incredible it is. That sense of purpose gave me confidence to start a life where I would go and meet people again. I had struggled to get out of bed in the mornings for so long, but I was suddenly packing my bag the night before and getting out before the sun was up.

When you're really ill, communicating is hard. What do you talk about when life feels unbearable? Talking about how cold it was when I was getting changed on the beach, or commenting on the waves or weather, helped me find my voice again. I found I was less twitchy and my emotions seemed to level out. I started to discover who I was capable of being.

In September 2019, I did a shout-out on Instagram inviting people down to the beach. I told them I'd hold a big pink pirate flag so they could find me. I told them they would be welcome, no matter how they were feeling. I think that appealed to a lot of people because nearly thirty people turned up. Before the first lockdown, there was one swim. By doing Zoom swim parties from baths filled with cold water, our children's paddling pools and wheelie bins, we came out of lockdown with thirty mental health swim groups ready to start. Since then, it's been a bit of a whirlwind. We have over a hundred swims now, nearly 300 volunteers and a little core team who support our swim hosts to create safe and welcoming spaces for people living with mental-health challenges.

However, the person I really welcomed in was myself. It's been an adventure over the last few years. I came out, I fell in love with an amazing woman, I stopped trying to shrink myself and started taking up space. I am a person with a complex mental illness, but it doesn't define me. I am living happily as a round peg now, no longer trying to fit in a square hole but instead feeling comfortable enough to just be me.

CONTRIBUTORS

Rachel Ashe is an outdoor swimmer, a fully fledged member of the big feelings club and an eternal optimist. In 2019, she founded Mental Health Swims, a UK-based organisation that celebrates the healing power of cold water and community. Back on dry land, you'll find her working with universities, mental health charities and environmental projects to champion kindness as the antidote to mental illness stigma.
www.mentalhealthswims.co.uk

Pauline Barker is founder of the Polar Bear Challenge and Devon and Cornwall Wild Swimming. Her passions are ice swimming, sea swimming and endurance swimming. In 2023, she was awarded an MBE for services to swimming in South West England.
www.paulinebarker.co.uk

Sara Barnes is a seasoned, all-weather outdoor swimmer and dipper based in the Lake District. She is an author and editor; her work has appeared in *Outdoor Swimmer* magazine and *The Island Review*, among others, and her book, *The Cold Fix*, was published by Vertebrate Publishing in 2022. Sara was featured in the 2021 BBC series *The Lakes with Simon Reeve*, sharing her love of wild swimming and the Lake District.
@bumblebarnes

Jo Clement is a free spirit and thinker with a rather simple outlook on life. She loves spending time in nature, camping, swimming, hiking, having spontaneous badly planned adventures and making memories with her small family.
*@jo_jo_clement_*
@cornwall_elopements

Lindsey Cole is a mermaid, cold-water swimmer, adventurer, environmental campaigner, author and a speaker. From mermaiding the River Thames to show how we're choking our waterways with plastic, to cycling the length of Africa to watch the World Cup, or retracing an incredible journey along Australia's Rabbit Proof Fence – Lindsey's a big fan of storytelling, exploring and campaigning for the environment.
www.lindseycole.co.uk
@stompycole

Loretta Cox is a Channel swimming coach and triple crown swimmer, but her best achievement is helping others realise their dreams and goals.

Anna Deacon is an author and photographer from Edinburgh who has co-written six books, including *Taking the Plunge* and *The Art of Wild Swimming* series, as well as the *Wild Guide to the Balearic Islands*. She has written for and published photographs in many national newspapers and magazines.
@wildswimmingstories

Ella Foote is a swim teacher, open-water coach, open-water lifeguard and year-round outdoor swimmer. She is the founder and director of Dip Advisor, an outdoor swim guiding business, and Editor of *Outdoor Swimmer* magazine.
@ellachloeswims

Beth French is an open-water swimmer and coach; amongst her many other achievements, in 2014 she was the first person to swim the twenty-six miles from Cornwall to the Isles of Scilly. Beth suffered with ME from the age of ten, ending up in a wheelchair at seventeen. She spent years learning from some of the world's leading indigenous practitioners about

the body and health and managed to forge her own path to wellness. She became fascinated by the potential locked within the human body and set out to explore her own inner horizons.
www.bethfrench.co.uk
@bethfrenchlives

Mikayla Guidera is an outgoing, always-up-for-an-adventure kind of girl. She is a huge advocate for mental health awareness and body positivity, and likes to spread good vibes and happiness on social media. Mikayla tries to live her best life as much as she can and always looks on the bright side of things.
@kayla_guidera

Hampshire Open Water Swimmers (HOWS) member **Wendy** is a content, calm lady who has found her happy place. **Lisa** is a group admin at HOWS; she encourages the ethos of taking troubles to the water so they can be left behind. Fellow HOWS member **Julia** is happiest swimming under an open sky, preferably at dawn when the world is at peace and the water is cold.

Stefan Hargrave is a dad of two girls, ethical banker and youth coach for Trojans Rugby Club. He also loves outdoor swimming.
@sjh_987

Simon Harmer – The Amputee Swimmer – is an open-water swimmer and inspirational speaker. He has tandem parachuted, cycled across America, swum Lake Windermere, and spoken to audiences across Europe; all this despite experiencing life-changing injuries as a result of an operational incident that cut short his successful military career. Simon is living his life as a 'thank you' to those who were there for him when he needed them.
www.simonharmer.com
@ theamputeeswimmer
@shorterSi

Emma Harper, also known as Mischief the Mermaid, is a freediver, ocean mermaid instructor, storyteller, performer and artist. She is the mother of three boys and a promoter of ocean conservation.

Johnny Hartnell is an avid wild swimmer who is usually found under a pounding Yorkshire waterfall or in a secluded river pool. Johnny's wild-swimming antics can be seen on Instagram.
@wildswimmingyorkshireman

Colin Hill is a Channel swimmer, has completed several two-way Windermere solo swims, is an International Marathon Swimming Hall of Fame inductee and has taken part in many open-water races and cross-ings around the world. He is the director of Ullswater Swim Place, and loves coaching swimmers from beginners to very experienced, as well as sharing his love for the open water.
www.ullswaterswimplace.com
@colin_hill_swims

Sarah Kennedy Norquoy is a keen outdoor swimmer living in Orkney. In her first book, *Salt On My Skin*, she tells of how sea swimming helped her come to terms with her mother's dementia diagnosis and the loss of a close friend. She describes herself as an 'unfluencer' and when she's not making people laugh she shares moving stories of her life caring for both parents with dementia.
@seasaltandsarah

Alice Kloker was born and raised in Minneapolis and enjoyed swim-ming in lakes from a young age. She rediscovered her love of being outside in the water over lockdown thanks to the friendly members of Hampshire Open Water Swimmers. Her outdoor swimming habit led her to a deeper awareness of the importance of water as a shared human resource and basic human right.
@AliceKloker

Dr Heather Massey is a senior lecturer within the School of Sport, Health and Exercise Science at the University of Portsmouth. In her spare time, Heather is a keen open-water swimmer, having successfully completed a

solo crossing of the English Channel and numerous other open-water swims, including relay swims round Jersey, Jersey to France and round the Isle of Wight. She also represented Great Britain in the World Ice Swimming Championships 1k event in 2017.
@H_Massey1979

Susanne Masters is an ethnobotanist and keen outdoor swimmer. She explores wildlife, landscapes, and culture on land and in water. Susanne is currently working on research on the wildlife trade; her book, *Wild Waters*, was published by Vertebrate Publishing in 2021.
@Ethnobotanica
@mastersmiss

Louise Owen is all about family, music, art and living by the water – beside the River Itchen. Until recently she worked in schools and colleges teaching languages, music and creative arts. She is now retired and is happily catching up on real life, playing in bands, making pictures and getting involved in local projects and environmental campaigns.

Beth Pearson is the editor of *elsewhere*, the free monthly online journal of the Outdoor Swimming Society, and co-director of the OSS.
www.outdoorswimmingsociety.com
@theoutdoorswimmingsociety

Les Peebles is an experienced wild swimmer and a wild-swimming guide, and introduces folk to the joys and many benefits of cold water in the Yorkshire Dales. He is passionate about helping others access this wonderful hobby in a friendly, fun and safe way. Most of his free time is also spent in the water around the Yorkshire Dales and Lake District.
www.thedalesdipper.co.uk
@thedalesdipper

Deb Phillips is The Sunny Mermaid, an open-water swimming coach; she is also an artist.
www.facebook.com/debthesunnymermaid

Katie Richards is a lone parent and divorcee who is building a new life back in her homeland of Cornwall and using the power of cold-water connection to create friendship and community.
@katieswimsandmakes
@swimminwimmincic
@newquay_merpod

CP Robinson is originally from the Midlands (almost as far from the coast as you can get in the UK); he now lives in Portsmouth and by day is Head of Corporate Partnerships for a children's charity. In 2021 he founded the *@Queer.All.Year* intersectional queer activism campaign and later joined the Portsmouth Pride Board of Trustees to develop campaigns and strategic work for all of the LGBTQ+ community. CP almost exclusively swims a variation of backstroke and is generally found on pebble beaches, but also enjoys a swoosh in a fast-moving river where swim buddies provide a helpful 'branch coming up on your left' shout in lieu of someone inventing swim rear view mirrors.

Sarah Shreeve is a teacher, a lecturer and a doctoral student. She co-founded Stop the Sewage Southsea, an activist group opposing sewage dumping into rivers and the sea. When she's not teaching or campaigning, Sarah can usually be found bimbling in the nearest body of water or eating cake.

Kate Steels is a winter swimmer, ice swimmer and open-water swimmer from Southampton. She is an English Channel solo swimmer, an Ice Sevens swimmer and has completed the 20 Bridges Manhattan Island Swim, among many other acheivements. Kate has been inducted into the Ice Swimming Hall of Fame and was the World Open Water Swimming Association's Woman of the Year in 2021.

Chris Thomas is the founder of the 365 Sea Swim Challenge, along with being an advocate for local marine conservation, community engagement and environmental projects.
www.365seaswimchallenge.com
@365seaswim

Catherine White is an actor, writer and gender expert for the United Nations.
@catherinejoywhite

Kathleen Wotton found her heart for living again and a drive to change her life expectancy through swimming in the sea. Her goal moving forwards is to keep doing what she loves and to reach out to a wider community through social media.
www.facebook.com/mermaidSeahamSlope
@seahammermaid
@ocean_calls_swimming

ABOUT THE EDITOR

Rachel Jones is a keen wild swimmer, a Mental Health Swims host, helps to run Hampshire Open Water Swimmers and is a member of the Friends of the Itchen Estuary and Stop the Sewage Southsea. She swims every day, enjoying the connection to nature as well as the cold water. When Rachel isn't swimming, she is a SEND teacher and a busy parent. She is also a keen photographer and credits swimming with helping to keep her sane and happy. She has completed the 365 Challenge, swimming outdoors every day of the year to raise money for charity. Rachel has written two innovative books on pedagogy; *Toes in the Water* is her first book outside that field. *@rlj1981*